# Letters to a New Minister of Education

## Fernando M. Reimers

With contributions from

Sergio Cardenas . Claudia Costin . Nuno Crato

Isak Froumin . Luis E. García de Brigard

Otto Granados . Eric Jamieson . Monal Jayaram

Igor Remorenko . Manolo Reynaud

Jaime Saavedra . Przemysław Sadura

Oon-Seng Tan . Kartik Varma

Cecilia Maria Velez White . Jerzy Wiśniewski

Shinichi Yamanaka

ISBN: 9781795182515

Library of Congress Control Number: 2019901076

Copy editing Ana Teresa Toro

Cover design Paulo Costa

# CONTENTS

iii

# Learning to Lead Education Systems

## Fernando M. Reimers

### 1. Purpose of this book

The purpose of this book is simple: to provide incoming Ministers of Education with a series of reflections from others who have held the same job, or who have worked closely with them. My hope is that these reflections on the practice of leading large-scale educational change will inspire questions, thinking and preparation that help those taking on similar responsibilities in the future learn from their predecessors.

Clearly, the context that each incoming Minister faces when they take on the job is unique in many ways. The opportunities and constraints facing the new Minister, whether resulting from the specific factors that demand educational change, from the level of resources available, from the level of public support for reform, from the institutional capacity of the sector, from the larger political context, or from the nature of his or her relationship to the President and other members of the Cabinet, create a unique situation. This is the unique 'mess' that each Minister will encounter and will attempt to make sense of. The first order of business for any incoming Minister to 'make sense' of the mess is to 'make sense' of their job and of the resources available to them to do the job.

'Making sense of the mess' involves turning a series of multiple interrelated challenges first into a series of organized and prioritized problems, and then into a strategy for action. This exercise in rational decision-making is embedded in a series of political and organizational considerations, such as how to define the problem and in whose company. Understanding how to influence those political and organizational factors is what I mean by 'making sense' of the job. No doubt, much can be gained from talking to as many well-informed people in the country in order to 'make sense of the mess'. But, at the end of the day, the responsibility to decide what to tackle and how, falls with the Minister. What support can Ministers find to discharge this responsibility? How can they make sense of the job?

I have seen many Ministers seek the company of fellow or past ministers at international meetings. I think they do it less to find technical solutions to their problems and more in hopes of finding kindred spirits from whom to learn how to make sense of the mess for which they are responsible and how to make sense of their job. There are, after all, already available analytic techniques which can be applied to the solution of problems, once those have been defined and prioritized, but there are comparatively fewer resources to help Ministers decide how to frame problems so they can be tackled, and even fewer resources to help them develop self-awareness and 'make sense' of the job.

2

When Ministers exchange experiences with other colleagues to 'make sense of the mess' they need to address, or to 'make sense of the job', they partake in a form of professional exchange that is essential to any profession. They reflect on their practice, invite colleagues to do the same, try to extract generalizable principles from which they can learn, and then offer those principles for scrutiny to fellow members of the profession. Those fellow members can in turn test those principles, by turning them into forms of practice that they adapt to their own contexts. In a sense, when a Minister approaches the job in a particular way, they are guided by a series of hypotheses about what a Minister can do, the power that they have, and how modifying those factors which they can influence will in turn change conditions which ultimately impact opportunities to learn and teach in schools. Acting on their hypotheses is akin to running an experiment. In fact, there are many smaller experiments embedded in the large experiment which is the strategy a Minister follows.

In a Handbook for Education Ministers[1] used in a Harvard training program for Ministers of Education in which I have been teaching for some years, I developed a tool to support

[1] Fernando Reimers, *Getting the Basics Right. Education*. This is a chapter in a comprehensive Leadership Handbook for Ministers which includes sections on Finance and Public Health (Cambridge, MA: Harvard Ministerial Leadership Program, 2018).

decision-making around the design of an education strategy, which structured the process in six steps[2]:

- Step 1: Select an ambitious the legacy goal.
- Step 2: Identify needs and opportunities for education improvement that relate to the legacy goal, and the root causes of deficient education outcomes or education needs.
- Step 3: Set priorities.
- Step 4. Develop a strategy to use budgetary levers to achieve legacy goals and outcomes
- Step 5: Identify pathways for delivery.
- Step 6. Plan for implementation.

But where does the knowledge that informs the hypotheses that shape such a strategy come from? Some of it comes from evidence about the state of the education system, some of it comes from research on the results of different ways to try to achieve various educational results, and some of it comes from the practice of having led efforts of educational change.

Some might wonder, given that there are already available powerful analytic techniques to generate evidence in

---

[2] The Harvard Ministerial Program, in which I collaborate with my colleagues Rifat Atun, Michael Sinclair, and other faculty from the schools of Public Health, Government and Education, is a program that builds leadership capacities for Ministers of Education, Health, Planning and Finance. The general framework I used to support an education strategy is the same framework used in the program to support a Public Health Strategy, though the specifics of how to carry out each of these steps obviously vary by sector.

support of policy and knowledge based on science that can help us tackle education challenges, what is the need for knowledge based on practice? Shouldn't a new Minister simply call on the best science-based knowledge and policy analysis and develop an agenda for reform based on that knowledge? The answer to this seductive question is simple: no! While science and techniques of rational analysis have much to offer those who need to make decisions about how to improve an education system, they are insufficient to determine which problems should be tackled and how this should be done. Developing and implementing effective education policies and leading an ambitious reform agenda requires highly specialized professional knowledge that must also draw on an understanding of practice.

In *The Reflective Practitioner,* a classic book on professional practice and education, Donald Schon argues that the ability to reflect on the knowledge which guides practice is essential to the improvement of professional practice.[3] Practitioners often guide their practice with problem-solving knowledge that goes beyond the mechanic application of principles or conclusions drawn from basic science. Schon also argues that the failure to comprehend this all too often leads institutions involved in professional education to base the curriculum on a paradigm which assumes that professional practice is simply the application of the general principles drawn from basic research in the field to problems of practice. I share Schon's view that such a paradigm is limited and insufficient

---

[3] Donald A. Schon, *The Reflective Practitioner. How Professionals Think in Action.* (New York: Basic Books, 1983).

to fully support effective professional practice, particularly when professionals encounter 'messy problems'.

Several scholars of leadership, including Peter Senge and Ron Heifetz, have made a useful distinction between the kinds of challenges leaders face: those to which the application of science-based technical knowledge can provide a straightforward solution and those to which it cannot. Senge calls the first kind convergent problems and the second divergent[4], and Heifetz terms them technical and adaptive challenges[5]. In a study of the relationship of educational research to policy-making and implementation, my colleague Noel McGinn and I found that the failure to distinguish between both kinds of problems accounted in part for the lack of use of research to inform policy change.[6] We proposed a recursive model of interaction between education research, policy-making and practice, which we termed Informed Dialogue, as a more apt way to align analytic tasks to the problems facing decision-makers, and the options available to tackle them.

Based on this recognition of the value of the often tacit knowledge which guides how practitioners think in action, I

---

[4] Peter M. Senge, *The fifth discipline : the art and practice of the learning organization* (New York: Currency/Doubleday, 2006).

[5] Ronald A. Heifetz, *Leadership without easy answers* (*Cambridge, Mass.: Belknap Press of Harvard University Press*, 1994).

[6] Fernando M. Reimers and Noel F. McGinn, *Informed dialogue : using research to shape education policy around the world* (Westport, Conn. : Praeger, 1997).

conducted a study of the practice of a group of education leaders who had graduated from the Master's program in international education policy at the Harvard Graduate School of Education. I surveyed this group of highly skilled professionals to understand what education challenges they were tackling, what impact their work produced, what obstacles they faced, what factors helped them address those obstacles, and what lessons they had learned from reflecting on their practice. In addition, I asked a subset of them to write extended essays on those questions. Based on the analysis of these surveys and extended written essays, I identified seven leadership challenges which these leaders working to improve education around the world face, which illustrate well the 'messy' nature of the challenges of educational change.[7] These challenges are:

- Educational challenges are complex, and capacity is limited
- The challenges are systemic
- Educational change takes time
- It's all about the people
- Mindsets matter
- Trust is key
- Fear can be a barrier

From the analysis of the practice of these education leaders, I drew ten principles which characterize how these leaders address these challenges:

---

[7] Fernando M. Reimers, *One Student at a Time. Leading the Global Education Movement* (Charleston, SC: Createspace, 2017).

1. Lead ethically.
2. Understand the education challenge you are trying to solve.
3. To understand the challenge, understand the people involved. Map key stakeholders.
4. Understanding how to solve an education challenge requires continuous learning.
5. Collaboration is key to learn and to act: There are opportunities in Collective Leadership.
6. Collaboration requires good personal relationships.
7. Attend to execution and to the details of getting the work done.
8. Communication is critical to learning and to execution.
9. Balance patience with setbacks and processes, with impatience for results.
10. There is a need for a different kind of education to support leaders.

The feedback and reflections I have received from education practitioners and graduate students on these leadership principles consistently point to the value gained from being able to consider –not necessarily mechanically accept– these principles drawn from studying the work of other leaders. In a graduate course on education policy analysis I teach at the Harvard Graduate School of Education, I receive similar feedback from my graduate students on the case studies included in the book *Informed Dialogue*, which are detailed analyses of a series of examples of interactions between researchers and policy makers in various countries around the topic of education policy. Similarly, my graduate students and I find value in the use of teaching cases in my graduate courses that present real examples of policy change, and in the education practitioners I bring to class as guest speakers to discuss the challenges they face and how they address them.

The theorizing of ways to relate the use of research to education policy reform based on analyses of case studies, the conceptualization of principles of education leadership based on the analysis of how practitioners talk about their work, and the use of the case method to teach education professionals, are all ways to help professionals in training learn how practitioners think in action. What these various approaches have in common is the recognition of the importance of practice-based knowledge to improve the training of future professionals.

This epistemological stance recognizes that when practitioners solve problems they learn from the consequences of their actions, and the knowledge they gain makes them better at solving problems in the future, hence better professionals. Solving problems, especially complex, messy, adaptive or divergent problems, thus requires much more than mechanically applying lessons drawn from research to new situations, and involves forms of creation, design of solutions, and experimentation. While good professionals learn from these private experiments that constitute their practice, this knowledge is often accessible only to the practitioner, because it is not processed in a way that allows others to learn from it. This is called 'tacit' knowledge.

Constructing opportunities to learn from such knowledge, of the kind illustrated earlier, transforms tacit knowledge into public knowledge and is critical to professional education. This is the role of a range of curricular and pedagogical approaches, such as apprenticeships, shadowing experts, receiving coaching from experts, and conversations with leaders of practice.

Some of the most fundamental critiques to university-based professional education concern whether the curriculum provides sufficient access to knowledge essential for effective practice, and whether such university-based professional education remains too theoretical and disconnected from the fields of practice for which it is preparing individuals. Donald Schon in *The Reflective Practitioner* argues that the classical model that sees practice as a mere application of foundational principles is responsible for this disconnect. It is not uncommon to hear voices from various fields of practice state that the deficiencies of professional preparation require that novices are taught what they need to know in the first years of professional practice. This challenge is compounded as technological change has increased the demands for professional practice in most fields, making clear that initial professional preparation is but one step in a long trajectory of development, that should extend throughout the careers of most professionals. Life-long professional preparation is recognized as essential to support people in their careers, especially as they take on new assignments for which their previous preparation and experience does not sufficiently prepare them, as is the case with most new Ministers of Education.

The utilization of knowledge based on practice as part of professional preparation is common in most professions. Medical schools, for instance, create a context in which apprentices can observe an expert and receive guidance from them as they solve real medical challenges when they engage students in clinical practice under the supervision of an expert doctor. Similarly, business schools use the case teaching method in which students grapple with real life or stylized business dilemmas, which engage students in a form of discussion of the world of practice from which they can develop the habits of mind to guide their own future practice. The use of the case method in law schools, similarly, is designed to teach those preparing to enter the profession to 'think like a lawyer'. In these and other professional fields, there is a growing industry of life-long professional preparation in which much of the knowledge that is gained is drawn from practice. At Harvard, new university presidents, for example, can attend executive education programs in which past or current presidents teach, as well as others who study the work of presidents. Similar executive education programs exist for new mayors and other elected officials, and for new presidents of companies.

There are multiple methodological approaches to draw knowledge from professional practice, including practitioners themselves engaging in reflection and analysis of their own practice. Many books used for instructional purposes in various professions illustrate this tradition. There is a cornucopia of books written by leaders of business organizations in which they reflect on their practice. Many political and business leaders, including former Presidents, contribute to a similar genre of memoirs which provide some access to how those individuals made sense of their past leadership efforts. Similar forms of reflection on practice are illustrated in books authored by teachers and other education practitioners, and there are various educational associations, such as the Association for Supervision and Curriculum Development and Learning Forward, that play an important role promoting the exchange of such practiced-based knowledge through publications and conferences.

Surprisingly, there are significantly fewer comparable means to share professional knowledge among senior education leaders of large scale system change, such as Ministers of Education or Superintendents of large school districts. The number of former ministers of education who have written books sharing what they learned effecting large-scale change is very limited, and certainly much more limited than the equivalent number of books written by business leaders, teachers, medical doctors or even Presidents.

Such paucity of knowledge based on the practice of large-scale educational systems change is unfortunate for several reasons. First, few activities could be more important to the future of a society than the education of its children and youth. Second, public education is often the largest social organization in a country, to which a significant level of resources is devoted. Given the importance of the activity of leading a national education system, the level of resources deployed by the sector, and the complexity of the task, there would be considerable benefits from the most professional exercise of such leadership. Arguably, throwing people into the job and hoping that they sink or swim is neither practical nor considerate. In order to professionalize this important activity, it would be highly valuable and useful to make the knowledge from those who have practiced the work well visible and accessible to others coming into the profession. This short book is a modest contribution to that genre. If the book engages the minds of incoming ministers, or of their advisors, and perhaps encourages others to write in the same genre, we would have succeeded in our aims in writing it.

The idea of writing the book emerged in one of the meetings of the Global Education Innovation Initiative (GEII). The GEII is a research and practice collaborative I lead with the aim of strengthening public education, so schools can better prepare students with the competencies necessary to participate, civically and economically, in societies which are rapidly changing as a result of technological advancements and of globalization. We carry out three types of activities in GEII. First, we conduct applied research on questions of interest to policy makers. The studies we have conducted include: (1) a comparative analysis of curriculum reform in six nations; (2) a study of the effects of entrepreneurial education programs in six countries; and (3) a study of teacher professional development programs designed to support teacher capacities to educate the whole child. Second, we organize and deliver "Informed Dialogues," which consist of convenings and expeditions designed to support learning among members of a group with a shared educational purpose. One of them was a learning expedition of 25 educators from Massachusetts that took us to examine how Singapore executes an ambitious curriculum for the 21st century, resulting in the publication of a book[8] in which some of the participants distilled the lessons they had learned and their implications for reform in Massachusetts. Another of these learning expeditions consisted of a two-day convening of a group of 50 education leaders to examine the challenges to bring to scale reforms that aimed to broaden the goals of the curriculum. This think tank resulted in the publication of a book in which some of the participants distilled what they had learned about such challenges, and their ideas to overcome them.[9] The present compilation of lessons learned by system-level leaders of educational change belongs in the same genre of literature. Finally, the GEII develops instructional materials to support teachers in designing effective instruction aligned with ambitious and rigorous goals.

A final word about what this compilation is and what it is not. This book should not be read as a recipe for education reform. It is not a step-by-step algorithm that a new Minister

---

[8] Fernando M. Reimers et al. *Fifteen Lettes on Education in Singapore* (Raleigh, NC: Lulu Publishing, 2016).
[9] Fernando M. Reimers et al. *Empowering All Students at Scale* (Middletown, DE: Createspace, 2017).

should follow. Rather, this book is meant to be a heuristic device, a series of meditations and reflections from people who have led reform efforts and which the reader should read as questions and as provocations for further thinking, not as answers that should be followed without considerable deliberation. They are meant to expand the range of perspectives that a new Minister brings to the job, in hopes that the exercise of engaging with and thinking through these perspectives will help the new Minister decide how to frame his or her job.

The people I have invited to contribute to this exercise are all leaders I respect for their capacity to be reflective, and to write an honest an account of what they have learned. Most of them are or have been associated with the Global Education Innovation Initiative, and the majority participated at the meeting where we discussed the idea of writing this book, and helped frame the purpose, content and tone of the project. The selection of the contributors also required that they had attempted ambitious education reforms. Whether those reforms succeeded or failed was not a selection criteria, rather knowing that these leaders had learned from their leadership efforts is what mattered. I suspect most of them will be the first to admit that some of the things they attempted succeeded and others didn't, but we can learn much from all of these efforts. I also invited leaders who could represent experiences in a variety of countries, so the book includes leaders of large scale educational change in Australia, Brazil, Colombia, Mexico, Peru, Poland, Portugal, Russia, and Singapore. Finally, by design, I invited a small number of people to write, in part to keep the book short so that it can be read by people who will have limited time because of the work that they lead.

These were the intellectual and epistemological underpinnings of this collation of essays. Those who were invited to submit a reflection on the lessons they had learned through their own efforts to lead large-scale educational change are in fact participating in an exercise of reflection on their practice. I realize the lessons they have drawn are at a high level of abstraction. It is not possible in these essays to see in any detail the direct experiences which inform the generalizations these leaders have drawn. As a result, the actual data or experiences from which these authors have drawn these principles are not observable or accessible to the readers of this book. Some might wonder, "Where is the evidence?" The evidence in this case are the conceptualizations of these leaders themselves and their own sense-making of their practice of leadership. My hope is that in reading across all the letters, the reader will be able to identify regularities or discontinuities, and then perhaps set out to test the emerging principles with his or her own experience and leadership practice.

Below are five principles drawn from my own reading of these letters, as well as from my own practice of three decades advising Ministers of Education and other large-scale system level leaders, and educating many generations of education leaders on the art and science of educational change.

**Principle 1. There is no change without implementation.**

There was a time when people thought that leading educational change was about making policy decisions about things like what to teach, to whom, in what way, with what technology, and at what cost. Implementation was often an afterthought, either assumed that it would happen or not of great interest to the decision-maker. In that way of thinking, policy-making was the domain of leaders, and execution was a separate domain of practitioners and administrators. Then practitioners and researchers discovered that implementation trumps policies and that the process of implementation can transform the best policy designs, often in ways which produce surprising and sometimes unintended results. I find this distinction between policy-making and implementation unhelpful, for there is no good policy if it cannot be implemented, and considerations that support implementation need to be part of the process of policy-making. A simple way to summarize this principle is: policies are intentions, and implementation and execution are what enable those intentions to produce results. Ultimately, a Minister is accountable for results, not for intentions.

**Principle 2. Leading large-scale change is a team sport.**

You can't transform an education system alone. There are so many people and groups involved in any attempt to change, that the first order of business is to develop a stakeholders map and to figure out a way to be in communication with them. Some of those groups are more visible than others, because they are in close proximity to the leader. The purpose of a map is to keep in mind all the stakeholders who matter, especially those who are less visible. A key stakeholder group in large-scale educational change efforts are students, because they stand to gain or lose the most from policies, yet they are very often invisible in the process of deciding what problems should be tackled and how. Similarly, teachers, who work day in and day out in classrooms, can either make or break a reform, yet are often invisible to leaders or claimed to be represented by representatives who are poor proxies for the views of teachers.

**Principle 3. Not everyone sees things in the same way.**

Mental models are key to help us make sense of which education challenges to tackle and how. Because leading change is a team sport, it is helpful to take the time to understand the mental models of various interlocutors the Minister will encounter. For instance, a most basic mental model is how we view the education system. One way to see the system is as an organization with the goal of helping students learn; this mental model orients towards improving the system's efficiency to achieve its goals. But the system can also be viewed as an organization of professionals with the expert knowledge to achieve the goals of the profession, and this mental model orients towards inclusion and creating opportunities for participation so that the collective wisdom of this expert community achieves its goals. An alternative mental model sees the education system as the largest public sector organization, touching just about every citizen in the nation; this mental model leads to political uses of the enterprise and to focus on improving the efficiency of the significant level of public expenditure devoted to it. Another mental model sees the very large number of students engaged by the education system as a market; this model leads to the creation of businesses to meet the needs of that market. Another mental model sees the education system as a means to prepare the younger generation to invent the future, and this leads to focus on scenario building and to imagining ways to improve society and make the future better than the present. Sometimes negotiations about education change are complicated because the framing models that various groups bring are different.

I have learned over the years that mental models can impede or support certain kinds of change. For example, much of my work advising governments has focused on improving educational opportunities for disadvantaged groups. There are various mental models conceptualizing educational opportunity. A very common model is what I call 'the elevator theory' to educational opportunity, which posits that educational opportunity is available when a student can access an educational institution in close proximity of the home. I espouse an alternative mental model which views opportunity as the factors that enable a series of transitions in the educational trajectories of students.

To these various mental models to conceptualize educational opportunity, we can overlay models about what is 'fair' or 'just'. There are at least three models of 'fairness'. One model of 'fairness' recognizes that schools are embedded in larger social structures and reflect those larger forces. That more advantaged children have access to more resourced schools is, in this model, natural and somewhat inevitable, and not something that should energize education reformers. An alternative mental model of 'fairness' sees each student as having the same rights, and therefore defines as 'fair' giving equality of treatment. Based on this model, unequal per pupil spending is 'unfair' and the job of leaders should be to try to equalize spending. Yet a third mental model of 'fairness' sees education results as the product of the combined role of school and other institutions, and posits for the school a 'compensatory role', to counter the influence of other social factors to produce equal educational outcomes. This model leads to efforts which are redistributive in nature, in effect giving more attention and resources to the most disadvantaged children. The complicated nature of negotiations about how to achieve 'fairness' in education among stakeholders with different mental models of what is 'fair' is self-evident.

Other mental models which I have found important in guiding leadership efforts include how people think of the relevance of education. Relevance of education relates it to a set of goals external to the education system, but which should these goals be – political, economic? When I propose that education efforts should be aligned with ambitious global goals, such as the reduction of poverty, achieving gender equity, and protecting the environment, this challenges an alternative model that views educational institutions as means to develop patriotism, or to prepare workers for existing jobs.

Similarly, people have different mental models about the locus of control for education results. Some people view educational outcomes as the result of factors which are outside the control of educators (poverty, politics, geography, culture); an expression of such external locus of control is the idea that 'poor children can't learn' or that 'they can't learn very much', a 'blame the victim' approach to explaining the often-evident low education results of children who live in poverty. An extension of this mindset is the refusal to learn from systems that have much better results because 'we are not Singapore' as if there was something in the cultural makeup of a nation that pre-determines how well students can perform academically. In contrast to this external locus of control, others see education results as the product of what education systems do, placing the locus of control for those results inside the education system. The job of leaders is often to increase the sense of internal control and self-efficacy, thereby increasing responsibility and accountability for results.

Another common mental model is whether we see education systems in terms of their deficiencies, or in terms of their strengths. Most education systems are neither a glass full nor a glass empty, but somewhere in between. Whether they are viewed as a glass half-full or a glass half-empty impacts how change is construed. In my experience, it is difficult to motivate people for a long time by creating a permanent sense of crisis and a mindset that 'the sky is falling', but

21

easier to do when a balance is struck between defining achievable goals, and recognizing achievements and progress.

Because an education system involves so many individuals, managing change is about managing people, so mental models about human nature impact the work of leaders. One mental model sees people as honest and trustworthy, as doing the best they can and know how to do. Another mental model sees them as self-interested and trying to get away with as little effort as possible. These alternatives views of human nature lead to different approaches to leading change that often have a self-fulfilling nature, because people can rise to our worst or best expectations of who they are.

The bottom line is that mental models about how the education enterprise works, about what is possible, and about how change works, are important to efforts to change systems. Often leadership will involve making visible these alternative mental models, and endeavoring to align various stakeholders within a set of shared mental models. It is helpful for leaders to be aware of their own mental models, to question them, and to consider alternative ways to frame the education system. A very useful exercise in mapping key stakeholders in a change process, is to map their mental models, not just their interests and power, as is most typically done in political mapping.

**Principle 4. Continuous learning and rapid adaptation is required.**

Trying to address messy problems is hard work, and requires continuous learning and rapid adaptation. Any policy decision is a hypothesis of the sort "If we do A, then B will happen, resulting in C". Reality often intervenes in ways which don't always conform to the original hypothesis. The sooner we learn how to adjust our hypotheses about how to make change happen, the better for the achievement of results. Leadership can either facilitate or impede such learning. One element in building a culture of learning is to create multiple opportunities for communication in which an inquiry stance is cultivated and supported. Encouraging others to ask why, to challenge assumptions, and creating opportunities to bring evidence to inform these conversations, will support a culture of inquiry. The book *Informed Dialogue* offers an approach to construct a culture of learning among the members of a change leadership team. Building a culture of learning requires investing in relationships, building trust, and creating multiple venues for communication and feedback. It is often recognized that leading change is largely about communication, but it is less often remembered that communication is not a one-way exercise, but an opportunity for many stakeholders to share what they know and to learn from one another.

A useful device to facilitate learning is to articulate the hypotheses which guide the change efforts, also called a 'theory of change', so that information can be collected continuously to confirm or disconfirm the key tenets of these hypotheses. Methodologies such as the Logical Framework Approach can help make visible the conceptual architecture of any education policy, program or project, and can guide a monitoring system that can provide feedback to continuously adjust the policy.

**Principle 5. Look to the future, with an eye to the past, keeping in mind that the world is changing.**

Education is fundamentally about equipping students with the knowledge, the skills and the dispositions that each generation considers valuable to conserve what they want to conserve, and to equip the new generation to build the future. This means education is simultaneously about conserving and reproducing culture, anchoring each generation in a sense of who they are that is firmly rooted in the past, while preparing them to imagine a better future, with the skills to bring it about.

Leaders of education change need to engage in scenario building to be able to contribute to helping individuals, communities and the nation, create a better future for themselves. But leaders also need to be rooted in history and culture: they need to have a sense of the history of the system they are leading, because much of the mindsets that intervene in educational change are shaped by that past and leading change is easier understanding the roots of those mindsets.

It is critical that leaders also keep an eye in the outside world, and on how it is changing. There is much to be gained from developing scenarios about our aspirations for the future in relation to the rest of the world, not in a vacuum. Educational institutions must empower global citizens to address global challenges and to seize new opportunities. Many predict that the Fourth Industrial Revolution, resulting from increased and ubiquitous automation and the development of artificial intelligence, will eliminate many of the jobs currently available. Together with neurotechnological and genetic developments, these changes will create new opportunities as well as serious challenges that require a heightened commitment to placing humans at the center and empowerment as an explicit goal.[10] A good referent for ministers are future scenarios, such as those developed by the World Economic Forum and published in the Global Risks Report. The Risks Report of 2018, for example, discusses a series of risks, in terms of likelihood and impact, and their interdependencies, such as risks resulting from weapons of mass destruction, extreme weather events, natural disasters, climate change, and water crisis, all of which would have significant global impact. Many of these risks are a function of human-environmental interactions, and those can be influenced through education. Yet, in many countries, these topics receive very little attention in the basic education curriculum, or even at the post-secondary level.

Keeping an eye on the evolving future needs to be balanced with a sense of history. The educational transformation experienced by humanity since the inclusion of education in

---

[10] Klaus Schwab, *The Fourth Industrial Revolution* (New York: Crown Business, 2017).

the Universal Declaration of Human Rights is one of the most significant silent revolutions in history. The world is significantly more educated today than it has ever been, and we should collectively take pride and be grateful for the construction of educational institutions around the world which enabled such a revolution to take place. Any incoming Minister is standing on the shoulders of the giants who preceded her and who contributed to building those institutions, and taking the time to understand and appreciate those efforts will provide not only a healthy dose of humility, but a valuable appreciation and understanding of the process of educational change. Some of the most successful ministers of education I have met are those who approached their job with the humility to appreciate the strengths in the legacies of their predecessors, and who built on those. Some of worst cases of failure I have seen resulted from Ministers who assumed that there was little of value in the institutions they had received, and who thought they could 'reinvent the Republic' during their tenure. As a wise Minister once told me, "I learned early in my tenure that every Minister reaps the fruits of what was planted by her predecessors, and plants the seeds of the fruits that will be reaped by her successor". Taking the time to study the existing programs and institutions may help sharpen that understanding of the long-term nature of the process of educational change.

A sense of time is also important. No Minister will have nearly as much time as they wish, and the time they have will go very quickly. You must develop a realistic sense of what can be accomplished in that time, and perhaps appreciate the importance of building on the efforts of those who have preceded you in the role. Lastly, you must remember that there is an urgency to serving the children, hence the need to prioritize and to pick one's battles.

I hope the reflections that follow in these letters generously written by colleagues who have preceded you in leading important large-scale efforts to improve education, will help you succeed in advancing the opportunities for the students under your watch to learn all that is possible to become architects of their own future.

# Lead with Ambition and Trust: A letter from down under

Eric Jamieson

*Eric Jamieson is currently developing and implementing an education strategy for GEMS in Saudi Arabia and Egypt, establishing a range of new schools to nurture education innovation and delivery from the school level through the national and regional levels. He has lead education reform at all levels. His most recent role involved guiding the development of an innovative initiative for Schools Plus, a major Australian not-for-profit. This role also involved leading schools throughout Australia in designing and developing creative new approaches to promoting profound change in the delivery of education for their communities.*

*In his previous role as Director of High Performance, he led the design and development of a high-order, possibilities-driven approach to strategic planning for the 2200+ public schools in New South Wales education. This approach was central to his vision of a powerful school growth model that aligned school planning, self-assessment, reporting and validation to create a self-driving system of improvement and accountability. The design was complemented by an innovative approach to school leadership, teacher quality, student learning, and assessment. It provided a low-cost, high-impact model as a catalyst for system transformation.*

*Eric served for seven years as principal at Plumpton High School in Western Sydney, beginning in 2004. During this time, he led the school through a complete transformation and reinvigoration, resulting in dramatically improved academic performance, student engagement, and attendance and retention rates.*

Dear Minister,

"In the face of an increasingly volatile, uncertain, complex and ambiguous world, education can make the difference as to whether people embrace the challenges they are confronted with or whether they are defeated by them". These are indeed very serious words posed by the OECD 2030 Education Program. They can be cause for inspiration or despair, depending on your belief in the possibility of achieving profound change in education.

Words of despair, for despite the best of intentions, there are very few Education Ministers or system leaders who can authentically lay claim to achieving transformation in education that best prepares for a changing world. Indeed, it is far too often the case that schools remain places where learning takes the form of a transmission of "packages of knowledge". Students are placed in the same disciplines that have featured in schools for decades. These disciplines are not connected to each other and lack authenticity in terms of application to the world in which students live. Assessing and ranking students on their ability to remember information and reproduce it in stressful test environments that do little to honor the rich and exciting process of learning still tends to be a key priority. In what other profession does the operating environment so closely resemble that which existed 30, 40, or even 50 years ago?

Words of inspiration, for society has never faced a greater opportunity to completely reimagine school education to be an experience that deeply engages a full range of learners in a way that gives meaning, purpose, relevance and connection. One that promotes imagination, curiosity, creativity and adventure, much like the exhilaration that happens through learning during the earliest years of our lives. Learning that is not contained within disciplines, but that challenges and demands that the learner go beyond the obvious, to combine a range of subject areas that help him or her to develop insights about the world's great wonders and challenges.

Given the importance of guiding, nurturing, inspiring and developing the young lives who will ultimately shape the future, there arguably can be no more important area for government focus than education. What a privilege it is to be in a position that can bring so much richness to our society through the wonder of learning for our children! The important question for you and for any educational leader to consider is, 'How do we best help every learner develop as a whole person, fulfill his or her potential, and help shape a shared future built on the well-being of individuals, communities and the planet?'

So, the great challenge for any Education Minister or system leader in our world today is how to radically transform an approach to learning that served an important purpose for an Industrial Age society, but that seriously lacks relevance for a rapidly evolving world. Given the familiarity of the current education approach for parents, teachers, system leaders, industrial organizations, journalists and politicians who have all participated in this type of schooling, the challenge is formidable.

Change rarely comes easily and transformation takes the challenge to another level, requiring leaders who operate at the highest levels of human consciousness. It demands vision, courage and imagination to rethink and redesign the way learning could and should be for the future. It requires leaders to mobilize a collective effort amongst all stakeholder groups, for them to be bold and liberate themselves from the familiarity of the known world of education as it was, so that together a new paradigm can emerge. This is no small challenge. Yet, to embrace a manifestation of learning that involves moving from following instructions to finding, framing and solving interesting and difficult problems, is the one way that we can build for a flourishing future. Andreas Schleicher, Director of Education and Skills at the OECD, captures this challenge through his question, 'How do we reconfigure the space, people, time and technology that can transform education?"

After an extensive career in education that spans six decades, including my own experience as a student, in addition to roles in teaching and as a principal, system leader, guiding a new NGO and as an international leader, I have been privileged to bring many perspectives to the gift of education to our world. In this capacity, I would like to share with you some advice that may be helpful to your thinking as to why, how and what is necessary to lead powerful educational change:

1. **Trust the profession.** The greatest asset you will have is a highly educated, intelligent, dedicated, passionate and determined group of people who are committed to one purpose – progressing student learning. If challenged and unleashed to create a greater manifestation of school education without the restrictions that have limited their work for decades, this group has the capacity to achieve profound change. They need to be trusted and enabled, as well as guided by a vision that inspires and elevates.

2. **Actively challenge the status quo.** You will face many who have been successful in the current education system and who see no need for change. It has served them well, so why wouldn't it do the same for future generations? Sadly, these people are often system and union leaders. They will claim that you do not understand the ways of education. Please challenge their thinking and ask of them, how can more of the same, even if tweaked, produce a different future?

3. **Dream big, knowing that anything is possible.** Throughout my experience, it is clear to me that adults and children alike respond best when recognized, valued, encouraged and inspired. A shift to meeting people where they are at and encouraging them to pursue possibilities without fear of failure or control, will truly enable them to be excited about learning each and every day. The power of the human spirit can produce

amazing things. Imagine a system where all teachers and students know they are trusted to learn, create and flourish together.

4. **Build on strengths rather than focus on gaps.** Education for many years has pursued a path driven by results based on unimaginative testing of narrow curriculum. It has featured a deficit approach where people focus on gaps, one with tight controls, restrictive frameworks, a bias to risk aversion, and often including demanding inspection regimes. These aspects have combined to focus effort on increasingly limited and prescriptive expressions of teaching, learning, management and leadership. By flipping the focus to people's strengths, and freeing education from the debilitating impact of heavy controls, they will themselves recognize those areas that they will want to develop to achieve authentic progress.

5. Above all, **trust your intuition.** Once the vision you wish to pursue is fully articulated, you will be in an incredibly strong position to know whether all that happens is aligned to the greater purpose of this vision and strategy. There will be widely divergent views presented to you through different ideologies. There will be those who resist change, others who need to be convinced, and still others who will be excited by the prospect. There will be a range of motives. Your task is to refer all positions and ideas presented to you using the greater purpose as your anchor point. All ideas, positions or challenges can be tested against this vision and purpose. Here, you will have your way forward.

My greatest wish for you is to appreciate each day that you are guiding the work of people who have entered a great profession because they want to make a difference to our most priceless gift, the young lives in their care. If the vision and purpose of your approach inspires them, if their roles in contributing to the vision are clear and supported, and if your approach authentically values, honors and enables them and the important work they do each day, they will achieve all you imagine and so much more. While all aspects of government are vital to promoting a flourishing society, the future of humanity literally resides with the young minds, hearts, bodies and spirits who can be inspired and enabled by the approach you lead and nurture. It is custodianship of the highest order, the greatest honor and the most unique responsibility.

I extend my deepest appreciation and very best wishes to you for the powerful work you will lead and for the rich legacy you will leave.

# How to ensure quality education in a very unequal city

Claudia Costin

*Claudia Costin is the Director of CEIPE- Center for Excellence and Inovation of Education Policies, a Think Tank within Getulio Vargas Foundation, a leading private University in Brazil where she is a professor. She was in the recent past a visiting scholar at the Harvard Graduate School of Education and Senior Director for Global Education in the World Bank. Before joining the World Bank, Claudia Costin was the Secretary of Education of the municipality of Rio de Janeiro. Under her stewardship, learning results rose by 22 percent in the city. She also implemented a strong Early Childhood program, working seamlessly across sectors with the Health and Social Protection secretariats.*

*Claudia has been vice-president of the Victor Civita Foundation, dedicated to raising the quality of public education in Brazil. Believing in the transformational power of education, she helped create the civil society movement Todos pela Educação, also serving on its technical committee. Convinced that teacher motivation is critical for real learning, Claudia communicates with thousands of teachers using social media.*

*She is also a member of the Global Commission on the Future of Work organized by ILO- International Labor Organization and she is a columnist in one of the leading newspapers in Brazil, Folha de São Paulo, writing about Education, Public Policies and Human Rights.*

As I was invited to the role of Secretary of Education of Brazil's biggest municipal school system, Rio de Janeiro, by the end of 2008, I was impressed not only by the scale of the system –1.063 schools, 700.000 students and 45.000 teachers– but also by the huge social and education inequality within the city.

Surrounded by many slums, or "favelas", as the cariocas call them, the difference in landscape in Rio reflected the learning outcomes of the children and adolescents that attended schools in diverse neighborhoods. The poor results in many of them were related to a combination of factors that affected learning: the low level of education attainment of the parents, many of them either illiterate or with very few years of schooling; the lack of teachers available to teach in hostile surroundings; and the overarching presence of a conflict linked to the drug-dealing business and the militias.

In addition to the vast differences in the educational outcomes of students of different social backgrounds, learning was not happening even in some of the best schools. In the national standardized assessment of student knowledge and skills administered in 2007 (Prova Brasil), only 29% of the students performed at an expected level in reading in 5th grade, a clear reduction from the level obtained in the previous administration of the evaluation, where 33% achieved comparable results. Unfortunately, the general perception was that this situation was only due to social promotion, a policy to reduce grade retention consisting of automatically promoting students from one grade to the next, which had been implemented some years before, which had the unintended effect of helping students progress across grades without learning.

The reality was far more complex. The problem was not only that students were being promoted without learning, it was mostly that the culture of low expectations resulted in insufficient acquisition of knowledge and skills, and students ended up held back at the 6th grade, where there was no automatic promotion and retaining students was allowed by the regulations, and then abandoning school after repeating the same grade two or three times.

Thus, two efforts had to be undertaken simultaneously: starting to build a culture of excellence and of high expectations for every student, and implementing affirmative action to ensure that the most challenged schools received additional support. The approach taken was inspired by Michael Fullan's recommendation of a systemic transformation when reforming the education in a city, so as to avoid fragmentation or the improvement of just some areas in a complex setting.

**Introducing a city-wide culture of excellence**

In 2009, as I started my work as Secretary, I knew that during the campaign, the then-future mayor of Rio had promised to end the social promotion system, that prohibited holding students in the same grade in a consecutive year at certain grades. Although I was convinced that repetition would not benefit any student, I thought it would be an opportunity to highlight learning, to ensure that students were promoted because they had learned and not despite not having acquired the skills and knowledge needed to progress academically.

With this approach in mind, my team and I developed a program based on the following principles:

- Schools should collaborate with one another, in an ecosystem of learning;
- Teachers should participate in the design of the curriculum, in the preparation of the textbooks to be used to support their practice, in the elaboration of the digital classes that were to be inserted in a platform to make teaching and learning more interesting, in the assessments, and in the elaboration of a remedial education course for the students who were not learning;
- We would open the system for experimentation, trying to find scalable good practices;
- Formative assessment would be incentivized and a unified test would be implemented in all schools every two months, with questions prepared collectively by teachers from different schools, to ensure that students were progressing as expected;
- Good teaching would be made visible, not only to the system, but to the whole city; and
- Equity and inclusion would be our most valued principles, alongside excellence.

The transformation started with the creation of a municipal curriculum, based on the skills and knowledge to be learned by every student and not just on content to be taught. Since there existed a general perception among teachers and parents that kids were not learning, we decided to start the school year with a general review, in all schools, of what should have been learned in the previous year and after 40 days, and we applied an assessment to know if there were illiterate students and to identify the learning challenges among the others.

To our dismay, we discovered that slightly over 28,000 students from 4th to 6th grades were still illiterate, which meant that we had to act quickly with them, so as to ensure they didn't leave school. To complicate this predicament, most teachers in these grades were not able to teach initial literacy to those kids while having to get the others up to speed. In addition to this challenge, we faced considerable age-grade disparity, with more than 22% of the students in 6th grade aged 2 years or more above the expected age for their grade. If these young people arrived at high school that much older than the expected age, chances were that they would abandon school at the first sign of failure.

Thus, we decided to create a system of remedial education that would include re-teaching basic literacy for students unable to read and write, with appropriate materials and specific professional training for their teachers. For the older kids, even those who were not illiterate, we created a process of acceleration in smaller classrooms and more dynamic and engaging teaching strategies which emphasized students' agency.

We were convinced that just building a curriculum and a strong system of remedial education would not suffice. The school journey was too short, and teachers were running from one school to the other to make ends meet and ensure a proper salary, with no time for collaboration and appropriate class planning. Excellence wouldn't be attained with just those initial steps.

It was important, as we were building an emergency plan to improve learning, to start to plan for a sustainable ecosystem of schools that could deliver quality education with high expectations for all and ensure better working conditions for the teachers. That was done by developing a plan to put, in twenty years' time, all the schools in one shift and starting to hire new teachers for 40 hours a week and not just 24 or 16 hours. As I left my position by mid-2014, to join the World Bank as senior director for Global Education, around 40% of the schools had at least 7 hours a day of schooling (including lunch) and just one shift.

## Improving equity in a school system that is being transformed

Since schools in vulnerable neighborhoods, especially in the many violent "favelas" in the city, were performing on average at a much lower level than other schools, some action was needed to ensure that the improvement would not benefit just kids from relatively better-off families. The transformation should affect every child and teenager in the city. That meant providing additional support for those schools, in a clear approach rooted in affirmative action.

In July 2009, we launched the "Schools of Tomorrow" initiative, that included actions such as:

- Paying more to teachers who would be working in these environments;
- Professional development for teachers and principals on conflict mediation and school climate;
- Providing health support (including mental health) for students in those schools;
- A special science program that involved much more experimentation in mobile science labs;
- After-school programs in arts and sports, with former students of those schools acting as workshop providers; and
- Promoting community engagement and making students agents of change in their slums.

With these additional supports, the schools were expected to, in time, narrow the gap in achievement and learning. In the beginning, the 155 schools involved had a dropout rate of 5,2%, much higher than the system average; the school's IDEB data, the national index for education quality, was significant lower  than the other schools.  In less than three years, the dropout rate was cut to 3,0% and the IDEB increased 33% in 9th grade (the most challenged grade for violent slums, since this is the age where drug-dealers and the militias tend to recruit their members).

Part of the transformation was due to the change in perspective. Teachers and principals were not just pitying those children, but trying to emancipate them, helping them to build a different future where their schooling would have a central role. Another component of the approach taken in those schools was that every pilot or experimentation in the system should start in one or many of the "Schools of Tomorrow". The reasoning was clear: if it works in a challenged school, it would work everywhere within the school system.

Thus, when we decided that it was about time to prepare a plan to increase the school journey, we replaced the two-shift system with one shift, and starting to hire teachers for 40 hours a week (including collaboration and class preparation time). We wanted to see how it would work in a slum, especially with the most innovative designs.

Thus GENTE –an experimental middle school– was created in Rocinha, one of the largest favelas, where we had taken advantage of the additional time for learning to pilot a more personalized approach which included a strategy to educate the whole child, with the support of technology. Similarly, in "Maré", another integrated group of slums, a complex of elementary and middle schools was built, organized as a campus, with the goal of optimizing resources and ensuring an appropriate environment for students and teachers.

Nothing was easy. While we were implementing those changes, conflict was emerging among factions and the police was invading the favelas, imprisoning the drug lords, so as to try to "pacify" the communities, in a process that seemed promising in the beginning, but unfortunately was discontinued some years later, after corruption scandals led the governor of the state, the vice-governor and some of his advisors to jail.

Unfortunately, later, the mayor, as the recession became evident in the country, decided to remove the extra payment of the teachers who were working in the "Schools of Tomorrow" and even the health program. But the experience has established a legacy, and even as successive Secretaries of Education had to deal with additional cuts in the budget and changes in the program, the "Schools of Tomorrow" have, if not remained as a program, changed the way teachers and students envisioned learning in fragile environments, with higher expectations for everyone.

**Building the conditions for the future of learning in the city**

In addition to the plan to ensure that schools could be more organized, with meaningful time devoted to not only give classes, but to educate the whole child and allow interactions among the students so as to ensure student agency and to foster global citizenship, we have invested in a strong early childhood education (ECE) program.

There was a relevant demand for vacancies in *creches* (early childhood education programs), but not a consistent pressure for quality at this level of education. The impression was that parents just wanted a place to keep their young children safe and cared for, while they work – which is quite understandable. But what we noticed, in the beginning, was that ECE centers lacked appropriate staff to educate and not just look after children, many of them from impoverished neighborhoods, where adolescent parents were not yet prepared to deal with the challenges of parenting.

We were sure that we should do three things at the same time, so as to level the playing field for these children and respond to their present and future needs:

- Hire real teachers with expertise in ECE, through a process that invested in the caretakers who were at the time working with them, offering them at least two years of pre-service education with emphasis on young children and recruit others with the appropriate training to fill in the gap;
- Build adequate infrastructure in or near areas of vulnerability to ensure vacancies for the most fragile families, with a lottery system that prioritized the recipients of Bolsa Familia (the Brazilian cash transfer system that addresses the needs of the families below the poverty line). For these families, Parenting Classes were also provided with the joint work of the Education, Health and Social Protection sectors within the city; and
- Create a municipal curriculum even for the babies and provide professional development and for every staff, including teachers and care takers, as well as toys and training in the organization of age-appropriate activities for these children.

More than 200 ECE centers were built and pre-service education was offered to approximately 2,500 caretakers who later took the public selection exam, approximately

1,800 of whom were hired as early childhood educators. Additionally, 3,200 were hired among teachers who were working in private schools or were just leaving university. With this effort in ECE, we believed that the educational disparities that originated from the differences in the social background of the older students could be diminished in the future.

The progress in the implementation of the one-shift schools and in the measures to ensure that every student encounters a powerful curriculum as well as a culture of high expectations is, in part, responsible for the fact that Rio's IDEB has been improving since that time.

Now, the approval of the National Curriculum, the *Base Nacional Comum Curricular*, will demand a continuous effort in professional development for teachers and a consistent monitoring of learning outcomes. With these changes, the system may have even better conditions to improve learning at a faster pace and further narrow the still-existing gaps in performance among student groups in the city.

**Lessons learned**

In advancing this ambitious agenda of educational change, not everything was smooth and tidy. A strong culture of low expectations was and, in part, is still in place. The idea that high quality education is only for rich kids who might aspire to continue to higher education is still prevalent. Additionally, some basic tools to build a better school are not yet there. Pre-service teacher education in the country is disconnected from the reality of the actual classroom and there is no solid culture of collaboration among teachers.

In fact, it is urgent to attract more talent to the career, as most education analysts in Brazil have already asserted. And for this to become reality, salary matters as well as social recognition for the profession. The narrative of victimization does not help the cause of teachers and only makes them less visible as good professionals, becoming more pitied than respected.

The pace of the reform was dependent on fiscal resources. Although salaries were improved in a significant way during my tenure, additional funding for better infrastructure became less available as events such as the World Cup and the Olympics consumed part of the budget and the fiscal crisis advanced. Definitely, local-level public education is highly dependent on decisions taken at other levels of government and even at the City Hall.

Another lesson I learned is the importance of constant interaction with principals and teachers. Since the beginning of my term as Secretary of Education, this was pursued, through the activation of a Board of Teachers elected from the school level up, that every two months met with me and my team to share their perspectives. A platform to disseminate good practices was also put in place (*Rioeduca*) and I also engaged in daily conversations on Twitter with teachers who wanted to connect and share their anxieties, criticism or suggestions about the educational changes.

This last tool was extremely helpful as a teachers' strike emerged, in the challenging context where every sector took to the streets all over Brazil, to complain about public transportation, health, education, and corruption. The constant dialogue did not prevent the strike, but helped in the negotiation process.

Looking back, it was a period of intense work and huge challenges, where I learned a lot. Now, when I talk to teachers, as I do almost every week through keynotes, panels or speeches, I am quite aware of how big the challenge still is, around the whole country, but also that teachers should be the main actors in a transformation that demands more of them than they may be initially ready to deliver. But no matter how hard the process of transformation might be, now with the new political context of the country, if society gets on board, we can do it!

# Letter to a new minister

## Cecilia María Vélez White

*Cecilia María Vélez White is the President of the Universidad Jorge Tadeo Lozano. She served as Colombia's Minister of Education from 2002 to 2010 and as Bogota's Secretary of Education from 1998 to 2002. She has also worked in Colombia's national Planning Ministry, Ministry of Foreign Affairs and Central Bank. She was the Robert Kennedy Visiting Professor at Harvard University and serves on several boards of education foundations and organizations.*

Dear new Minister of Education,

I know that the challenges you will face in improving your country's education system are unique, due to the way in which the sector has developed, the enrollment rates, the quality level, the government you are part of, and the political support you have, among other factors. However, I am going to share with you some thoughts based on my experience having been Minister of Education of Colombia for eight years which I hope will be useful to you. Some of the key achievements during my tenure included that we developed a program that increased enrollment at all educational levels, we developed a quality improvement system, and we modernized the management of the sector.

51

There were some conditions that made possible my continuity in the government and the consequent implementation of the programs. First of all, I want to underscore my personal attitude vis-à-vis the job. I acted as if I was going to be at office enough time to make the changes I wanted, but I was also ready to quit at any moment if the conditions were no longer propitious. This disposition was important because it allowed me to undertake difficult actions without succumbing to short-term pressures, but with the awareness that, if necessary, I would step down. This attitude was liberating, allowing me to take the steps and make the decisions that needed to be made, even when they were unpopular.

Initially, it was important to analyze and take into account the available information about the sector, the statistics, and the research (national and international), to set realistic objectives and to have a reference framework. Then the key task was to define the priorities through the design of a development plan for the sector: objectives, policies, strategies and projects. To do so, I got support from external experts but mainly relied on the team that was going to put in place the plan. It was crucial to define the implementation details: the way we were going to execute and follow up, the people in charge, the specific procedures, and the moments for evaluation and assessment of progress.

At the Ministry there are always countless demands that arise from different actors: government, Congress, institutions, community, and the media, all of which need to be addressed. However, you must keep focusing on the strategy and not to get lost on firefighter tasks. If the plan you designed effectively tackles the main needs of the sector, it is most likely that those demands have already been considered in the plan. You can then take advantage of individual demands to check if the plan's implementation is useful in a particular situation and to explain the policies to the different actors.

Maintaining strategic focus was especially useful to me in dealing with members of Congress whose demands were generally about individual problems, around a municipality, a school, or a teacher. I always used those individual cases to explain the importance of the general policies that would address them and others like them.

To maintain focus it is important to establish routines of monitoring, discussion and evaluation with the team. I had a weekly meeting with the executive team, and they had a weekly meeting with their working groups. It was important to respect that time on the calendar, even when it was challenging to do this because of the many demands on our agenda.

It is important to have early achievements. In my case, during the first year of government, these where: first, the increases in student enrollment due to a better use of the physical plant; and second, the payment of overdue debts to teachers. These accomplishments allowed us to work with less public pressure upon the projects with long-term results and gave us governability.

We had the strong conviction that it was crucial to undertake an institutional change that allowed the sector to obtain the results that were set in the plan and to make the change sustainable. An important chapter of our plan was focused on aligning institutions to their objectives. The parallel structures (that may be necessary to start a project) are ephemeral and do not guarantee long-term actions, which is the work needed in education.

To successfully work with institutions, we placed individuals committed to the objectives of the administration in key positions, with the capacity to lead the institution to implement the plan (using delivery strategies including project planning, human resource management, monitoring procedures, and performance indicators, among others). It is important to take into account the organizational knowledge available in the sector: their previous performance, their key strengths and weakness, and the loopholes.

Additionally, in our experience, it was very effective to integrate other actors in the plan implementation, like NGOs working in education, private educational institutions, and civil organizations interested in the sector. They were included in the policy discussion and as project implementors. We encouraged public-private initiatives. The integration of those organizations enhanced the capacity of the public sector.

Communication is a key element in leading large-scale change. This is true for all governmental efforts, but it is crucial for education because the results depend on the behavior of multiple actors including institutions, teachers, principals, students, and parents. It is important to guarantee a fluid communication with the sector, the organization, and with society in general. We created a high-level committee to define the content and the approach to communications, be they situational or policy-related. The committee met weekly and was led by me, with Ministry directors and external advisors participating.

Communication with teachers is always critical and it is useful to create forums and other spaces in which to discuss policies with them. In the Colombian case, since there were already annual local and national forums defined by law, we used those existing spaces and strengthened them. The unions were a good channel to address teacher work conditions, but were not the best channel for other issues such as policy or pedagogy discussions. Additionally, we used communications strategically during crises (especially if they involved public opinion) to deepen public knowledge of our policies. During my time in government, and more so now, the Internet and social media were not only effective means to communicate the policies and actions of the Ministry, but also helpful to listen to and consider different viewpoints.

Last but not least, transitions are important. The continuity of the main goals and actions will depend on the documented information that your successors receive. We dedicated a considerable amount of time to documenting what we were doing, the objectives that we had accomplished, and the way we achieved them. We did that in teams with the participation of the people who were going to remain at the institution. We also spent time preparing the hand-off of the Ministry to the next team.

And finally, be a good predecessor. It is important to have in mind that education is a long-term strategy, and the continuity of the policies depend on how your successors understand your achievements beyond political considerations. A good relationship with them can help the development of the system.

I wish you good luck during the challenging and rewarding experience you are going to tackle. Luck always helps!

# There is no downside to humility

## Luis E. García de Brigard

*Luis E. García de Brigard is an educational entrepreneur who has founded multiple organizations including Enseña por Colombia, Volunteers Colombia, Appian Education Ventures and Envoys. He served as Deputy Minister of Education of Colombia and has been a member of numerous boards of educational organizations in Colombia and the United States.*

I left my position as Deputy Minister of Education of Colombia after a short but incredibly intense tenure. We had managed to secure the largest budget for education, surpassing that of defense for the first time in the country's history. Colombia was pushing through the final stages of peace negotiations with the FARC guerrillas which would put an end to over five decades of conflict. In this context, investment in education was gaining relevance in the public agenda as a new avenue for building the country's future.

This unique juncture allowed my team to pursue a series of ambitious reforms that aimed to jumpstart the system. We introduced a new index to measure educational quality, modernized the process to recruit new teachers, and reformed their in-service evaluation. We introduced curricular reforms, put in motion a plan to end double shifts

57

in schools, and raised the largest school infrastructure fund to date. At one point, however, I was so exhausted –or so I told myself– that I decided to resign.

In the next couple of years after my departure from this post, I entertained the same narrative: I did my part, left it all in the field, and departed when the job was done. Mission accomplished. I intentionally isolated myself from the public sphere and focused on my private sector endeavors, even turning down the President's offer to rejoin his cabinet as Education Minister. Not long after, however, I started to see with concern that some of our flagship reforms were losing direction or being abandoned altogether by new administrations. This sparked a deep period of reflection about my leadership, what we had attempted during my tenure, and about the future of education in my country. I humbly share some of my reflections in the hope that they can help others who are faced with the challenge and privilege of leading educational systems in their own countries.

**They won't take my idealism.**

After much reflection, I concluded that it was not exhaustion that drove me to leave the Ministry. I had not lost my energy. I had lost my idealism. The demands of the job (the long hours, the opposition, Congress, unions, public exposure, etc.) had slowly eroded my conviction that a better world is always within reach, that battles for justice and equity are worth fighting for, and that sacrifices are necessary if we are ever going to achieve quality education for all children. The void was quickly filled with cynicism. Dirty politics, bureaucracy, incompetence and corruption became easy excuses to rationalize the failure of the system and my own choice to leave it.

Idealism, however, is the most powerful source of motivation that an educational leader can have. It is the idealism of a handful of leaders that has driven access and opportunity for billions of children around the world. It is idealism that invented free, public education. It is idealism that has fought exclusion of the weak from educational systems. It is idealism that continues to attract young students to become teachers and devote their lives to the service of others. Cynicism, instead, has little merit to claim in the phenomenal advancement of education that humanity has accomplished in recent history.

The public sector can be a phenomenal opportunity for idealists to build a better world for future generations. Paradoxically, it can also be a dangerous threat to idealism itself. Years after leaving office I made a promise: I won't let them take my idealism away. To those who have chosen to serve I say: don't let them take yours.

**Posters don't last forever.**

The modern political sphere is obsessed with communications. The public sector is generously staffed with communications experts and consultants with lofty budgets. The rationale goes that effectively communicating policies to the greater public is, in fact, a form of public service. Education is no exception. Ministries and districts around the word invest billions of dollars to inform the public about their programs and reforms, and in doing so, they often aim to improve government approval ratings and, in some cases, the popularity of the Minister. We were no exception. Our programs were cleverly named, their graphics beautifully designed and their content actively aired during prime time. We had logos, jingles, posters and slogans to communicate our efforts. Posters, however, don't last forever.

After leaving office I realized that the ephemeral excitement that comes about through flashy communications is not enough to ensure the survival and longevity of educational reforms. I came up, after the fact, with what I called *the endowment test*. This test consists of the following: in designing educational policies, ministerial teams must ask themselves if the reform in question is likely to become one that is dearly cherished by parents, students, teachers and the society at large, or if it can be sustained only by the influence of power or marketing. If the former, the policy is likely to endure time and administrations. If the latter, it will likely evaporate as soon as their champions leave office. If there is one thing in common among high-performing educational systems, it is that they have become part of the social endowment of their respective countries, one that citizens are proud of and will protect against the volatility of politics. Reforms can be fueled by smart communications. True legacies take much more than that.

**It's all true, but it's not all the truth.**

I come from a technical background and my team did too. Trained at some of the best universities in the world, we embodied the classically overconfident young team that thought they knew it all because they had read it all. We had actually read a lot. For every policy under discussion, we cited studies, journals and results from randomized control trials. We were an email away from the world's best renowned educational experts and institutions. Technocracy at its best. In our minds, nothing could be better than this scientifically informed, data-driven approach to educational leadership. I won't lie. This served us well. We were able to iterate quickly, avoid mistakes, and better tackle the challenges facing the system. However, this approach missed a critical element. While the literature that accompanied our efforts was sound and robust –in other words, true– it could not capture or explain *all* of the challenges and realities that we had to address. Papers and data are, by definition, limited in their scope and reach. Extrapolating them to every possible situation or context hinders one's disposition for genuine and humble inquiry; for listening, observing, and learning. It traps you into thinking that the certainty that *something* is true is equivalent to knowing *all* the truth.

No Minister and no Ministry will ever know the whole truth about the challenges, realities and contexts that they face. Children are best served by leaders that combine the discipline to know what is known with the humility to learn what is not.

## Ethics beat tactics

Educational systems are, by nature, large and complex. They involve many and very diverse stakeholders and are characterized by tensions and conflicting interests. Negotiating and mediating conflict is thus inherent to the job of system-level educational leaders. My work was, in that respect, extremely challenging. I was responsible for the largest budget in the country and was therefore bombarded with pressures that ranged from bureaucratic appetite to outright corruption. I led negotiations with the teachers' union, a 300,000-strong organization with enormous power and influence. I managed the relationship between the national-level Ministry and 95 regional secretariats of education with diverse challenges, capacity and agendas. In addressing these complex scenarios, I instinctively resorted to well-studied negotiation tactics, game theory and power dynamics. Every negotiation was preceded by long strategy meetings and densely scribbled whiteboards. However, during the endless hours that I spent at the negotiating table, I learned that complex environments –such as those that characterize educational systems– can suffer from *tactical overload.* There is a limit to outthinking and outsmarting; to bluffing; to displaying power; to making and assessing threats and promises; to secret and backdoor negotiations.

I found no better strategy to negotiating and mediating conflict than pure and simple ethics: honesty, transparency, the absence of hidden agendas or personal interests and, most importantly, genuine concern for students. In my experience, this *high road* approach to negotiating conflict consistently yielded better outcomes for all parties. Education, after all, is humanity's greatest example of value creation. It should therefore never be approached as a zero-sum game.

Common to all these lessons is the notion of humble leadership: one that is disciplined and rigorous but open to listening, learning and making sacrifices. Arrogant, entitled and overconfident leadership can yield short-term political results but will never serve the children in the classrooms. The best antidote against the blinding thrill of power is remembering that humility has no downside.

# Systemic education reform through distributed leadership:

## Seven Things to Do

Monal Jayaram and Kartik Varma

*Monal Jayaram is a Core Team Member and Program Director with Kaivalya Education Foundation in India, an initiative of the Piramal Foundation for Educational Leadership. KEF is a change management organization that supports leadership development of state leaders, district leaders and school leaders to improve student learning outcomes. She leads the Centre of Excellence for Social and Emotional Learning, Teacher Leadership, School Leadership and Assessments. She is an esteemed member of national and international committees which focus on developing qualitative pedagogical curriculum and examination patterns with a holistic approach to human development. Along with other authors from the country, she has contributed in GEII's books Teaching and Learning for the Twenty-first Century, Educational Goals, Policies and Curriculum from Six Nations, and Preparing Teachers to Educate Whole Students: An International Comparative Study, published by Harvard Education Press. With over 20 years of expertise in the field of enhancing pedagogy levels through tools and techniques, she seeks to enhance the skills of school educators to make learning more meaningful for children.*

*Kartik Varma is a Core Team Member and Program Director with Kaivalya Education Foundation in India, an initiative of the*

*Piramal Foundation for Educational Leadership. KEF is a change management organization that supports leadership development of state leaders, district leaders and school leaders to improve student learning outcomes. Kartik is part of the leadership team for PFEL's State Transformation Program, which works with 10 states across India for systemic education reform. He also leads the Centres of Excellence for Learning & Development and Organization Development for the program. Prior to joining PFEL, Kartik spent 17 years in management consulting across India, MENA and Malaysia, advising clients in multiple geographies on issues like digital government, talent management, organization growth and restructuring strategies. He has written and spoken on issues like the future of work, building leadership pipelines, and creating next generation entrepreneurs. He holds a Global Executive MBA degree from INSEAD (Singapore, France & Abu Dhabi) and has held advisory positions in multiple NGOs in education.*

India has 140 million children in the primary education system today, about 10% of its population. One of the most important challenges of our times is to drive large-scale change in the education system, quickly and with high quality. Since Independence, the focus has been solving the issues of access and equity. This fifty-year journey has yielded significant dividends: today, enrollment is above 96% and the drop-out rate for girls has steadily declined (*Source: ASER 2018*).

While the country was making progress on these issues, however, the very future of work has been changing. The future of work we are actively creating requires our children to be skilled in collaboration, creativity, maker skills – a completely different order of skills from the numeric and literacy skills government institutions are designed to deliver. Governments worldwide are thus grappling with a fundamental contradiction: our children deserve meaning, learning, joy and pride to flourish in the future; the people and education systems that are supposed to deliver this are usually built on the exact opposite premise: control, 'inspection', 'top-down', 'authority', 'task'! How do we create and build distributed leadership across levels within these institutions, such that our children will have role models for what the future of leadership looks like? Untangling this Gordian Knot is the daily challenge of multiple governments, systemic officials and others around the world today.

The experience around the world (including in India) points to seven specific things that governments can do to shape institutions by building distributed leadership. No surprises here: it all comes down to people. To be clear, multiple countries are experimenting with different models in pockets. However, a large-scale, speedy and sustained drive remains elusive in many countries.

1.  **Hire the future you want:** Entrance tests for teachers are usually well-defined and assume some degree of professional qualifications. However, there are two significant gaps emerging:
    a.  The selection processes are largely subject-specific. Little or no assessment is done for the real classroom leadership capabilities of these individuals. The critical abilities of asking open-

ended questions, active listening, non-violent communication and influence rather than instruct are not a criteria at all, and instead are left for post-hiring (if at all). This contradiction becomes even more surprising when we reflect on the fact that we all 'know' that this is the kind of teacher we want our kids to be introduced to.

b. The selection processes for middle and senior management officials (systems-level officials) is similarly missing an assessment of leadership capabilities. For the teacher workforce to sustainably demonstrate leadership, the support of leaders at every level is an essential condition. Additionally, unlike any other endeavor, the act of teaching has moral purpose at its core – and a bureaucracy that is not anchored culturally around that often ends up with being focused on the transactional.

It is clear that selection processes across these cadres must shift to deploy leadership assessments as a pre-requisite, not as a 'nice-to-have' element. Creating and deploying a 'multi-stack' competency framework that selects for 21st century skills is the first and most important sustainable driver of behavior change across institutions.

2. **Induct right:** Induction is the moment of truth for any new team member. Often the assumption is that pre-service training or qualifications are sufficient to cover

the basics for any teacher or systems-level official. Experience and data suggest this is a missed opportunity. Teachers and systems-level officials are often left to fend for themselves, with little knowledge of leadership capabilities, ways of working/teaching, or a chance to refresh their skills. The result is an 'accidental culture' where employees learn the ropes and their leadership styles emerge as a mirror of the constraints and limited paradigms of the past. A structured, 'First 100 days' kind of induction program provides inputs on behaviors, skills and knowledge essential to the job, its context and its stakeholders.

3. **Build leadership capabilities, 'real time, all the time':** There is a clear need to have teachers and systems-level officials who demonstrate a growth mindset and continuously seek to learn new things so that they can do their jobs better 'on Monday morning', and who create a genuine 'learning organization'. This is the heart of the distributed leadership paradigm that allows for reduced control and supervision, and delegated authority and capabilities to solve problems at every level. Only with building these leadership capabilities can institutions have leaders who can trust themselves and others to achieve a common education objective.

It is critical for governments to start allocating budgets for much more than workshops that happen once a year or have no clear linkages to on-the-job performance. A sustained, 'omni-channel' approach to building leadership capabilities in teachers and systems-level officials would merely reflect our lived reality today:

mobile devices, internet and free online resources have made 'continuous learning' a fact of life. Gone are the days when our kids used to learn only in classrooms or only from a teacher. It only stands to reason that as adults, teachers and systems-level officials also will learn through multiple sources, including professional learning communities of peers and projects.

However, the key is to not try to build all capabilities all at once. Our experience suggests that building a critical few capabilities or behaviors is the only viable option for large-scale transformation. This is, therefore, a multi-year journey and requires clarity, focus and continued investments.

4. **Build the leadership pipeline:** The next step is to provide clear career progression frameworks that allow teachers/systems-level officials to grow, manage greater complexity, and unlock more of their own potential by solving newer problems. Currently, teachers/systems-level officials are largely stagnating at certain grades/levels with little hope of promotions and growth. Promotions are largely based on tenure and come around once in a decade. The result: a disengaged and demoralized workforce that has no incentive to solve complex problems.

Providing lateral and vertical career progression will also help talent to be more fungible across long-existing boundaries of the multiple institutions that usually exist at state levels. It also allows for individuals to design their own careers in a sense, which again reflects the increasing reality of the future of work.

5. **Smarter, more human processes:** eGov and its more recent form of digital government is reducing repetitive, paper-based work in every area of government. In education specifically, the volume of administrative tasks usually outweighs academic work by a ratio of 2:1. The institutions and their work processes are usually chronically under-staffed, managing multiple government schemes and all of this is manual. Teachers and systemic officials end up spending more time on actions related to access and equity, rather than quality. In many cases, the individual optimizes for the 'flavor-of-the-month', and academic support and focus are the usual victims.

Additionally, in more litigious systems, the teachers/systems-level officials are spending valuable time defending themselves in courts of law, and additionally avoiding courageous decisions that risk more litigation.

The answer seems to lie in focusing on a few key administrative processes that take up significant leadership attention and automate, optimize or eliminate them. However, in the spirit of building leadership capabilities, it is not merely about reducing paperwork or replacing one faceless process with a faster one. This is also about making these processes more 'human-centered' so that the process owners have the right degree of distributed authority to take decisions on the ground. This is also the chance to reallocate work away

71

from administrative tasks to focusing the entire bureaucracy on key academic tasks.

These process improvements, updated workflows and supporting systems become the most institutionalized and sustainable way to build newer leadership behaviors everywhere.

6. **Coach, don't manage performance:** Performance management systems in many governments are characterized by the need for compliance, control and achievement of 'standards'. While this certainly allows for transparency and proper usage of public funds, there is an urgent need to include genuine performance 'management' and coaching, which maximizes the potential of teachers/systems-level officials across levels. When done well, everyday coaching represents a living example of great leadership behaviors. Right from the senior bureaucrat to the classroom teacher interacting with the students, coaching forms the essential and missing link today. Setting KRAs that focus on outcomes and behaviors has been used for many years now in various governments. The additional need today is to include newer behaviors, and transition from annual reviews to real-time feedback.

**Building institutional capacity to deliver capacity:** All the above initiatives apply to systems-level officials, as we have seen. This is at the core of building the next generation of education leaders. This is widely understood, but not well executed in many parts of the world. Often, the focus on delivering capabilities for the teacher with the limited budgets/resources available misses the opportunity to deliver results sustainably. The results are high vacancy rates across levels, poor capabilities and weak processes within these institutions. For the senior and middle management to be able to appreciate, participate and further the education goals, governments must invest in the right strategy, workforce, capabilities and systems of the institutions that are charged with delivering these mandates.

The problems of access and equity are not gone, and governments cannot take their eyes off the ball. However, the future is catching up quickly with us, and we can no longer delay the urgent need to create the next generation of leaders, at scale and within our lifetime. Many countries have embarked on this mission for many years now, as they continuously reposition themselves within the global economy. The seven levers detailed above working together are aimed at building the future leadership grammar and capabilities of the institutions and schools that are tasked with delivering the coming generations of the workforce. Adopting and putting this agenda front and center is a key responsibility of the coalitions that exist at multiple levels today.

# Issues to keep in mind when planning and implementing large-scale reforms that broaden the goals of the curriculum

Shinichi Yamanaka

*Shinichi Yamanaka is Chairman of KADOKAWA DOWANGO Education Institute. He is also an Executive Adviser for education at the Hiroshima prefecture. He was Japanese Ambassador Extraordinary and Plenipotentiary to Bulgaria, and Vice Minister of Ministry of Education, Culture, Sports, Science and Technology (MEXT). Shinichi has also worked for MEXT as Director General of the Department of Elementary and Secondary Education, Minister's Secretariat, and the Department of Sports and Youth. Other roles he has occupied include Councilor of the Cabinet Secretariat, as well as Deputy Director and Director of the Committee of Education Reform and the Committee of Education Rebuiltment. He was also Chairperson of the TALIS Governing Body, OECD. Shinichi has also been an Associate Professor in the Graduate School of International Economy at the Yokohama National University (Intellectual property rights), and an Adjunct Lecturer in the School of Education at the University of Tokyo (Education policy).*

Based on my experience with educational change, the following six principles can help create space for significant education reform and support it.

## 1. Establish a committee for discussion of national education reform

When trying to make fundamental educational reforms, it is important to conduct a nationwide debate on education, to carry out such reforms based on what is learned in such debate. In general, people prefer improvements to solve problems in front of them, rather than making fundamental reforms. This is also true with respect to educators. Therefore, when education reforms are to be carried out at the national level, it is important to set up an ad hoc committee with a wide range of members including the business and the labor community, rather than just including educators, to obtain broad support to an ambitious educational reform plan. Particularly with regards to curriculum reform, it is important to discuss what the competencies and skills are required to participate in the society now and are likely to be necessary in the future, from the viewpoint not only of educators, but also of people in industry, science and technology, globalization, and demography. These conversations must examine the gap between the ability of students who graduate from school and the competencies expected by the industry, and examine how education needs to be reformed to close this gap. This kind of dialogue should be the starting point for education reform in this rapidly changing society.

## 2. Develop a standard national curriculum

When implementing curriculum reform to introduce 21st century education, the existence of national or state-level standard curriculum is beneficial to support implementation. It is important to include educational methods as well as educational goals and contents to support 21st century competencies and skills, such as students' ability to utilize knowledge in real life, ability to learn, and ability to accomplish tasks in collaboration with others.

However, it is difficult for teachers to change their practice simply as a result of reading about new teaching methods in the standard curriculum. Basically, teachers are good at teaching knowledge but are not so good at teaching how to learn or how to utilize knowledge. Therefore, in order to support teachers in mastering new teaching methods, they must have access to new courses in which those methods are used. While practicing new teaching methods in special courses, teachers will be able to master them and then transfer the use of these methods to lessons in other subjects. Printed and digital materials explaining new teaching methods to teachers, providing materials of model case collections, and holding workshops and seminars can also support improvements in teachers' instructional practices.

## 3. Conduct nationwide assessments of academic skills

To carry out reforms, it is imperative that stakeholders understand the urgency to the current educational situation. It is difficult to implement reforms if the key parties do not have a sense of crisis about the current situation. The sense of urgency increases in society when it becomes clear that students' academic ability is low compared to other competing countries. In some countries, the results of the PISA assessments from the OECD have triggered educational reform. Establishing a national academic achievement exam would be also an effective tool for clarifying the educational situation both at the national and regional level. Also, when undertaking fundamental curriculum reform, it is necessary to create a system to verify what is being improved by the reform. It will take some time before a test to evaluate competencies and skills required in 21st century is made available. In such a case, PISA would be a good model to evaluate such kind of academic abilities.

Although academic achievement tests can be an important means for broadly and socially understanding the situation of education, it is also important to think about the adverse effect of tests. Once it becomes evident which areas and schools achieve at high levels and low levels, the schools with high levels of achievement will become more popular and attractive to more motivated parents, which can set in motion a reinforcing mechanism in which the schools with good results become better, and those with poor results decline even further. In this case, the use of assessments could broaden educational inequality among schools and regions. It is therefore essential to clarify what kind of support would be provided to schools where it becomes evident that students perform at low levels.

## 4. Professional development system

New educational methods are needed to implement the new curriculum. It is important that teachers are confident about implementing new educational methods before they stand in front of their students.

An initial training system should include teacher training programs to prepare teachers to cultivate 21st century competencies and skills, such as critical thinking and creativity. Continuous training and a robust support system for teachers to learn new teaching methods is also important. It is important that teachers have opportunities to learn and understand the new curriculum and new teaching methods through teaching materials, training courses, and workshops. The use of ICT in teachers' training programs is important.

To understand the new teaching methods, teachers must have opportunities to take courses deploying the same instructional approaches which they are expected to use, so they can experience their effectiveness directly. The ability of teachers to implement the new curriculum is key to the success of the reform.

## 5. Enhance school-community partnerships

To deliver an education that fosters the creative thinking and creativity of students, it is also important to cultivate the ability to utilise knowledge in the real world. To implement 21st century education, it is important to promote community and parental involvement in school education. School and community collaboration include the participation of local volunteers to support school education as teaching assistants, giving students opportunities to take internship programs in companies. It is important to establish a mechanism in which both local communities and parents are involved in shaping the goals of schools and educational policies, to enhance cooperation between school and society.

It is important to make meetings at national, regional and school levels, to assess the results of the education reform and refine further implementation. Discussions should be based on actual data, such as the results of achievement assessments or surveys measuring employers' perceptions around the preparation of new graduates entering the workforce. Since everyone can discuss anecdotally and based on their own experience, there is always a risk that discussions are biased by the individual experience of the members of the meeting, so the use of data is critical.

## 6. Money

It is true that money changes everything. Also, it is true that money can change education, and education changes everything. But we face difficulties when we try to increase budgets for education competing with other fields, such as public works and agriculture. Public support is essential to increasing budgetary support for education. In this respect, a nationwide consensus on the importance of education spending is critical. School-society partnerships are also important to helping society understand the challenges and difficulties of schools and what schools need. To realize fundamental educational reform and to get enough money for it, it is necessary to gain the understanding and support from society.

# Reflections from a Secretary of Education to his successor at the end of his tenure

## Otto Granados

*Otto Granados served as Secretary of Education of Mexico from 2017-2018, and as Deputy Secretary for Planning, Evaluation and Coordination from 2015 to 2017. He also served as Ambassador of Mexico to Chile, Governor of the State of Aguascalientes, Deputy Secretary of Planning, Press Secretary to the President, and Chief of Staff to the Secretary of Education. He chairs the advisory board for Education, Science and Culture of the Organization of Ibero-American States, and serves on the boards of numerous educational organizations.*

Recognizing the challenging nature of the education issues governments must tackle, the urgency to tackle them, and the cost of making mistakes, those who have been in senior leaderships roles often want to share some of what they have learned with their successors. I will share some of my views here, among which there will be a combination of thoughts –inevitably ambiguous– around achievements that should be defended, valuable lessons, experiences, and, of course, insights about failures and frustrations. Far from endorsing any particular course of action, I would like to share some reflections with those who are about to take office as Ministers of Education in any reasonably democratic developing country, under presidential regimes with sensible political leaders.

## 1. Ask the right questions.

Almost every new government, whether it arrives with abundant, medium or minimal political support, has a natural maximalist tendency. What I mean is that they will want to reinvent the country and start radical changes in the short presidential terms that are typical in countries where immediate re-election is not allowed: for example, in 1982, when the Socialists won the general elections in Spain, one of the new ministers promised that they "will change the country to such an extent that not even their mother will recognize the country".

In education, as well as in other sectors such as health or social development, instant radical changes are impossible for several reasons, including that there are many people involved in the sector, and that achieving results takes time. The  transformation of education systems will be achieved only through long and slow processes. So, if you are just arriving to your new post in the Education Ministry, try hard and ask the right questions about issues like school enrollment, educational quality, or conditions affecting social and economic mobility. In fact, ask yourself what you want to achieve at the end of your term, and how you would like to demonstrate your achievements, ideally through measurable, comparable and reliable data. This is what incumbents will ask at the end of your term, and how the next government will evaluate your work.

## 2. Spend your political capital at the beginning of your term to make difficult decisions.

Unlike economic or financial markets, where you are always looking to increase and save your own resources, the opposite should be done in politics: you must spend your political capital at the beginning of your term, when this capital is possibly at its highest, to make difficult –but important– decisions, even if they are unpopular. The explanation is simple: your political power will vanish quickly, your incumbents will be cruel and brutal, and political circumstances will likely change. According to a study conducted by the Inter-American Dialogue, the average term of a national Minister of Education between 2000 and 2015 was barely over two years, so do not get any false hopes. Out of the hundreds of different educational reforms implemented in the last fifty years, with diverse aims and scopes, those that did not cause tensions and conflicts were very unusual, mainly because real reforms affect the vested interests of unions, bureaucracies, political parties, legislators, and even NGOs. Indeed, a reform without conflict is not a reform. If you are serious about starting a systemic or structural educational reform in your country, you must be aware of the timing, because in politics, as the saying goes, "the postman never rings twice".

## 3. Politics, not policy.

In almost every policy domain, but especially in education, there are almost as many academics, "experts" and "specialists", as there are students or teachers. Walter Mondale said in 1971 that in education policy "for every study, statistical or theoretical that contains a proposed solution or a recommendation, there is always another, equally well documented, challenging the assumptions or conclusions of the first." He was right. You have to learn, listen, analyze, compare evidence, and review data, but in the end, remember that the prevailing rationality is politics. Politics, and not policy, is what matters to achieve your goals. Therefore, trust your common sense.

**4. Governing is budgeting.**

Whether we like it or not, the main role of a leader is to define priorities and allocate resources. In the field of education, especially in emerging countries, there is a huge misconception that equates a bigger budget with better educational results. This is not true. Indeed, to fall into that trap creates perverse incentives for bureaucrats, who will then assign resources inadequately. Poor results will be a consequence of allocating resources to educational levels with the lowest social rates of return, or because public officials decide to spend public resources mostly in salaries. You should reject this misconception, and promote the idea that in any decision regarding educational expenditures, spending wisely should prevail over increasing expenditure.

**5. Build broad and effective coalitions for change.**

Educational systems in emerging countries –or to be very clear, the political, bureaucratic, or union structures that usually capture those systems– are by definition very conservative. They are used to enjoying the *status quo*, to living within a predictable and favorable ecosystem where they always get benefits, to capturing public resources and taking advantage of the influence they have to determine teachers' careers. It is not true, as some novice ministers believe, that teachers are defenseless, and that they depend exclusively on the government's generosity to achieve some progress. The main challenge is to articulate political, media and civil coalitions willing to consider that short-term instability is a small price to pay for a real change, and that it is worth supporting the real transformation of any education system. In fact, if the reform you promote actually shakes things up, it would mean that it is going in the right direction. Even more, you should try to create the right incentives, to get support from citizens despite how problematic the implementation of a reform might be.

**6.   There are no shortcuts in educational transformation.**

Since the international debate around cross-national assessments that started about two decades ago, with the administration of tests like PISA, TALIS, PIAAC, and different national assessments, almost every Minister of Education has to deal with a depressing period after results from these tests are shared with various constituencies, letting them know that their education systems are not at the top of international rankings. As expected, any Minister of Education would like for his or her country to be among the top performers while they are still in office and to enjoy some political dividends from their efforts. Unfortunately, this is often impossible, due to several reasons. First, transforming any national education system will take at least 20 to 30 years, and no political calendar is able to sustain such a period of time. Another reason is even more important: educational goals cannot be measured simply by tests, but through the achievement of economic and social mobility for every student during their lives. Mobility can be a consequence of access to a good education, and it can have an impact on national productivity, competitiveness, and economic growth, but assessing whether these gains have been realized is only possible in the long term.

## 7. Innovation and improvement alone are not reinvention: continuity matters.

After a government turnover, incoming officials have a natural tendency to communicate that everything from the past is terrible, and that rainy days are finally over. This is never true. In fact, promising immediate improvement is suicidal, given that designing effective public policies overnight is impossible. If this is true for any field, in education it is still more evident because improvement processes depend upon long policy cycles and require a constant and well-organized distribution of inputs for extended periods of time. Thus, the main challenge is finding how to improve policies and programs already available in the national education system, and describing these efforts as part of different policies.

## 8. Cycles of government: friends, allies, competitors and enemies.

If you are planning to be a good Minister of Education, please forget about your own political aspirations. At least in the case of Latin America, for the last five decades no

Minister of Education has become President, with two exceptions maybe, and one of those for completely accidental reasons. Giving up your political intentions will provide you with a great advantage, because other top public officials and potential candidates will not consider you a political competitor or an enemy, but a friend and ally, supporting all your endeavors. In fact, there are two actors in government who should be your main allies. One is your own boss: if the President does not respect your opinion, makes inefficient or absurd decisions regarding educational policies, or restricts your own freedom, you are lost – either because he knows more than you do about educational policy, because he does not share your vision on education, or even because he simply does not care about what you recommend. In any case, you are lost. If this happens, pack your bags. Your other relevant ally is the Minister of Finance. To that Minister, you may be the third or fourth priority, probably after the sectors of public safety, infrastructure, or health. But for you, as the Minister of Education, he or she is the most important ally you should have.

9. **Every benefit or cost resulting from the education reform must be clearly communicated.**

Unless you are a cynic or do not actually care about educational progress, from the very beginning you must be honest with your constituencies. If your goal at the end of your term is that improvement in national tests be visible, or that more people experience social and economic mobility, or even just that perception of improvement in the education system is visible (even if this perception is hardly measurable), your obligation is to visualize and define goals that are achievable within a period of only a few years. You must be clear about the fact that building an excellent educational system (that eventually could be one of the best in the world), will take many years and a series of government administrations. Promising otherwise, just to obtain short-term political benefits, is plain deception.

### 10. Forget your political campaign.

More than twenty-five years ago, the management guru Peter Drucker published some rules that, according to him, Presidents should follow if they really want to succeed. He recommended that they should not stubbornly do what they wanted to do, but to accept real political contexts; to concentrate and not splinter; to understand that an effective leader is aware that there is no risk-free policy, and to put in practice the advice Harry Truman gave to the newly elected President John F. Kennedy: "Once you are elected, you stop campaigning".

# Lessons from Mexico: How to think politically about reforming a national education system

Manolo Reynaud

*Manolo Reynaud* served as a senior official in the previous administration in Mexico (2012-2018) and supported an ambitious education reform at several stages: first, during the post-election transition phase in the autumn of 2012, when the initial version of the bill was drafted; from 2012 to 2015 as an aide in the President's office; and finally, from 2015 to 2017, as senior advisor to the Secretary of Education. He is a graduate of the London School of Economics and holds a master's degree from Oxford University.

It is often said that those who fail to learn from history, are doomed to repeat it. While specific historical circumstances may never be recreated, studying them can no doubt point to useful lessons. Similarly, although every education system and its context are different, the recent Mexican experience may be valuable to others who are attempting to transform their country's education.

In 2012, an ambitious national reform was launched only days after the last government's inauguration, as part of a wide-ranging reform program based on a rare multi-party consensus. In essence, this reform sought to move beyond what had historically been the state's main focus, namely ensuring sufficient *coverage*, in order to improve the *quality* of education. In other words, the newly stated aim of the education system would be to equip all children, regardless of social origin, ethnicity or gender, with the knowledge, skills, attitudes, and values they would need to achieve their personal and professional development, and contribute fully to society in the twenty-first century.

To accomplish this goal, the reform sought to revamp the curriculum, both for K-12 education and teacher colleges, emphasizing critical thinking, complex problem-solving, and socioemotional development. At the same time, it embarked on a major drive to consolidate a strictly meritocratic professional career ladder for teachers. Furthermore, it sought to transform the historically vertical and rigid organization of the Mexican education system and to diminish the significant power of the teachers' unions.

The new governance model involved new actors more actively (the students' families and local communities, civil society, local authorities and the independent *Instituto Nacional para la Evaluación de la Educación*, among others) and progressively empowered schools, while developing their capacity to use their growing autonomy responsibly. Finally, the effort set out to address historic inequalities by targeting resources to the most disadvantaged groups in society.[11]

---

[11] For further reading on Mexico's 2012-2018 education reform and its various components refer to the bibliography.

As one would expect, such an ambitious package of changes encountered strong resistance among vested interests, especially from the teachers' unions – so much so, that in last summer's presidential elections, the newly-elected president campaigned on a platform to undo much of it out of both ideological and more practical electoral considerations, most notably the meritocratic exam-based career ladder for teachers. What eventually happens to the reform remains yet to be seen and its final merits will be for others to judge.

## 1. Always put students first

The first lesson is that, whatever the circumstances one finds oneself in, the main priority of any reform effort should be the students. As obvious as this may sound, when dealing with the political and policy intricacies of implementing a complex reform, it is easy to lose sight of this overarching goal. It really is useful to pause every now and then to ask oneself if one's efforts in fact contribute, whether directly or indirectly, in the short-, medium- or long-term, towards improving students' learning. If one cannot honestly answer that question affirmatively, then it is time to reassess priorities and reassign resources accordingly.

In Mexico's case, the current education system was created in the early twentieth century with a corporatist vision to ensure political control of the population. While this guaranteed stability of labor relations and allowed for rapid growth of the number of schools and teachers, the system was not designed to support improvements in teaching or learning. Captured by political, bureaucratic and union interests, over time this arrangement bred high levels of inefficiency and corruption, oblivious to the educational needs of students.

That is why the recent reform sought to reorganize the entire educational system to align it to the learning needs of today's students. The central slogan of the reform was: *Primero los niños* (children first). Explicitly putting children at the heart of the reform movement was not only crucial to maintain focus, but also very powerful politically. Especially at the height of the conflict with the unions, it was always helpful to remind the public in general and the students' families what was at stake. In more than one instance, including in those regions where the union was the most radical and militant in its opposition to the reform, the pressure exerted by concerned parents was key to sustaining the momentum for change.

## 2. Listen to a diversity of voices

The second lesson is that one should always listen to a great diversity of voices. It is very common for people, be they citizens, policymakers or teachers, to think about education in terms of their own experience as students, knowingly or not. That is why it is vital to listen to a great diversity of voices: people at different levels and in various areas of the education system, including those who have held one's position in the past or those who are doing similar things elsewhere, but also the vast number of specialists dedicated to education outside the system.

This is especially true when one is not a specialist in education, but it also holds true for leaders with prior experience and expertise in the sector: to keep one's mind always open to other points of view, that is, as a reality check which can help avoid costly mistakes. Thus, one should never stop visiting schools and listening to teachers, principals and parents, as well as to experts, union leaders and other policy-makers (particularly those with different opinions).

In the Mexican experience, the initial reform proposal was developed by taking stock of the ongoing debate and listening to practitioners and union leaders of all political persuasions, as well as independent specialists and academics. The draft was then subjected to intense discussions between the leadership of the main political parties of the left, center and right. Once approved, the bill itself mandated the government to conduct broad public consultations to revamp the education model, which it did in a first round during 2014 and then more extensively in 2016, with the support of the *Centro de Investigación y Docencia Económicas*, a prestigious Mexican academic institution.[12]

In addition to getting a more complete picture of the education landscape, listening is key in identifying ongoing processes of implementation. No matter how deep a change one is planning to effect, it is crucial to remember that

---

[12] This report was published in early January 2017 (Heredia, 2017).

education systems are not only complex, but in constant flux. At any point in time, at various levels, endogenous and exogenous forces are affecting the system and it is very important to understand at which precise moment one is entering the scene. In many cases. there will have been relevant efforts before one's arrival. Understanding one's place in that long succession of changes is vital to increase the chances of success at reform.

For example, when Mexico's recent reform was launched in 2012, significant changes to upper secondary education had been under way since 2008, with the aim of harmonizing the historically heterogeneous subsystems. As a result, even though the education reform was initially focused mainly on primary education, in the process of internal and external consultations it expanded its scope to incorporate the reorganization underway in high schools. This paved the way not only for the next generation of changes to upper secondary education, but also ensured that the primary school reform was aligned with them.

### 3.   Choose your battles carefully

The third lesson is that one should choose one's battles very carefully. While education systems are *dynamic* in the sense that they are constantly changing, the pace of that change is slow. This is due in part to the fact that education systems are often large and complex, with decentralized structures of governance as in Mexico for instance, where the federal government shares the responsibilities of public education with local authorities. There are also cultural reasons, such as the tendency of educational institutions to be conservative and mostly reproduce the dominant culture and norms, rather than to innovate. Under these circumstances, changing –let alone reversing course– is extremely difficult and costly.

That is why it is so important to invest heavily in early and careful planning. A successful reform requires a very clear long-term vision, but also strategies for the short- and medium-term based on a realistic appreciation of existing financial, human and political capacities and constraints. One of the aims of the Mexican process, for instance, was to make the education curriculum completely bilingual – Spanish and English speaking– while also preserving indigenous tongues. Yet the existing English-teaching capabilities were so limited that the decision was taken to focus the equally limited financial resources on the training of the next generations of English teachers.

It is often said that for education reform to be effective it needs to be *comprehensive*. While this may be true in the sense that different components of the system are closely interlinked (e.g. the curriculum and teacher training), one should not succumb to the temptation of trying to fix everything. It is vital to identify exactly what levers are the ones that trigger the structural change one seeks and to choose one's battles accordingly, sequencing the proposed and necessary changes. In the recent Mexican experience, despite being a very ambitious effort to reform many aspects of the education system, there were clear priorities which also meant postponing other urgent reforms. Two examples of such (still) pressing issues are the financing of public higher education institutions and the concentration of schools to combat the historically huge (and inefficient) dispersion of physical and human resources.

While the policy challenges of implementing an ambitious reform are numerous, the political obstacles involved are often even more formidable still. This means that, in the same way one needs to plan the sequence of the various stages of policy reform, it is also critical to think politically about low-hanging fruit to offer to the public while the long-term benefits of reform come into effect. Asking teachers, parents and public opinion in general –and of course the opposition– to be patient and have faith in the education leaders, will simply not do.

In terms of communication, this means that many times the most transcendent elements of a reform process in terms of policy and long-term change may not necessarily be the ones that should be emphasized in the messaging about the reform. Some issues may either be too complex or too far-removed from people's daily concerns to be effectively communicated and to mobilize support. Others still, might be too sensitive politically to be aired in the public arena and would be better dealt with discretely in closed-door negotiations with the interested parties.

As part of the recent Mexican reform, for instance, an unprecedented effort was launched to refurbish and equip tens of thousands of schools, starting with those in the poorest regions of the country, financed by infrastructure bonds issued at the Mexican Stock Exchange. Improving the physical conditions for learning was no doubt an urgent necessity, but it was certainly not the core element of the reform. And yet, because of its immediate and tangible benefits for students and teachers, it was stressed significantly as part of the communication strategy.

## 4. But once you have chosen your battles, fight them with conviction

When one gets involved in reforming education, a common recommendation is to involve stakeholders at all levels and strike alliances with relevant actors. As a matter of fact, institutions can hardly change against the will of the people who constitute them (e.g. a curricular reform will not be implemented without the support of teachers). In that sense, one of the most important tasks to initiate change is indeed to reach out to stakeholders to start a dialogue and build alliances. Now, as desirable as a broad consensus on the goals of reform would be, one needs to realize that this is not always possible. In fact, in many cases the interests of various groups are in direct conflict so that one cannot promote change without producing losers and the natural resistance this entails.

Again, Mexico's recent experience serves as a case in point. The government's most urgent challenge was to regain control over the education system, which was largely captured by the teachers' unions, before it could start to undertake changes properly related to instruction at the school and classroom level. In other words, the first part of the education reform was really a political reform of the education system. Clearly no amount of dialogue and negotiation with the various fractions of the teachers' unions could ever change the crude reality that vested interests were going to be affected and inevitably try to resist the changes (and resist they did).

If choosing one's battles and planning for them with care is always important, it is particularly so when those battles involve a significant level of conflict. In these cases, when reconciling interests and reaching a consensus "across the aisle" is not possible, it is crucial to ensure cohesion within the coalition of allies one has, starting with full political and budgetary support from one's own party and government. Likewise, from the vantage point of an Education Minister, it is key to ensure the reform's mission and sense of purpose are shared throughout the Department in order to overcome the silo mentality so prevalent in bureaucracies.

## 5. Conclusions

Someone once said that there are many people who can teach a good class and others still who might run a fine school, but there are precious few who will succeed in building a great education system. Progress is rarely linear and the cycles of democratic politics may sometimes hurt even the noblest of causes. Since the costs are usually felt before the benefits, opponents tend to be more vocal than potential allies. Initiatives that are beneficial in the long-term may be sacrificed prematurely. And yet we need to keep trying.

In today's interconnected world, as technological innovation keeps accelerating and changing the way we live and work at an unprecedented rate, education is the foundation for a person's and indeed a nation's success. That is why, more than ever before, countries need to make sure that their schools are preparing future generations for the challenges they will face.

Finally, on a more optimistic note, it is worth bearing in mind the power of *precedent*. Even when reform efforts face resistance from vested interests, and do not have the time to mature and realize their full promise, in the long-term they are valuable for the simple fact that they serve as precedent. For as the political pendulum swings in one direction, it may eventually swing back the other way.

### References

Granados Roldán, O. (2018), *Reforma educativa*, Mexico City: Fondo de Cultura Económica.

Guevara Niebla, G. (2016), *Poder para el maestro, poder para la escuela*, Mexico City: Cal y Arena.

Heredia Rubio, B. (ed.) (2017), *Consulta sobre el Modelo Educativo 2016*, Mexico City: Programa Interdisciplinario sobre Políticas y Prácticas Educativas (PIPE) - CIDE.

INEE (2015), *Reforma Educativa. Marco Normativo*, Mexico City: Instituto Nacional para la Evaluación de la Educación and Cámara de Diputados.

Mancera Corcuera, C. (2018), "La Reforma Educativa: su pertinencia, implementación y perspectivas" in Granados Roldán, O., Puente de la Mora, X. and Betanzos Torres E. O. (eds.), *Fortalecimiento de derechos, ampliación de libertades.* *Volume I,* Mexico City: Fondo de Cultura Económica, pp. 26-124.

Nuño Mayer, A. (2018), "Respuesta a *nexos*. La reforma educativa" in *Nexos* (491), pp. 18-21.

Reimers, F. (2018), "Reformar la escuela pública para el siglo XXI. Los desafíos para México" in Granados Roldán, O., Puente de la Mora, X. and Betanzos Torres E. O. (eds.), *Fortalecimiento de derechos, ampliación de libertades. Volume I,* Mexico City: Fondo de Cultura Económica, pp. 125-166.

SEP (2017), *Aprendizajes Clave para la Educación Integral. Plan y programas de estudio para la educación básica,* Mexico City: Secretaría de Educación Pública.

SEP (2017), *Modelo Educativo para la Educación Obligatoria. Educar para la liberta y la creatividad,* Mexico City: Secretaría de Educación Pública.

# Should you talk to the "experts"?
# Advice for a new Secretary

Sergio Cardenas

*Sergio Cárdenas is an Associate Professor in the Department of Public Administration at the Center for Economics Research and Teaching (CIDE). A former director the Regional Cooperation Center for Adult Education in Latin America and The Caribbean, he has been lead researcher in diverse technical cooperation projects. He is also part of the Global Education Innovation Initiative, and Editor of the journal "Reformas y Políticas Educativas", published by Fondo de Cultura Económica.*

Educational researchers sometimes ambition the findings from their own research projects be used by decision-makers leading educational systems

Starting a conversation with leaders who have in their hands critical decisions that usually affect thousands or even millions of students is undoubtedly a personal and professional challenge for any researcher. It is especially true if a researcher is trying to sensitize or adequately inform decision-makers about problems that have prevailed for years in a school system.

Despite how intuitive it might sound to consider these types of conversations useful for public officials and researchers alike, the reality reminds us that achieving this is usually complicated. These conversations, whether public or private, happen more as an exception than the rule. "Healthy cycles" of the use of evidence in which solid research has a direct effect on the design of educational interventions is not as frequent (or easy to achieve) in practice as theory suggests.

Of course, there are multiple explanations for this situation. The natural mistrust of those who point out what they consider are errors is proportional to the one that exists towards those who are assumed to commit them. The lack of understanding of the slow timelines that prevail in academia parallels the lack of understanding of the haste that usually prevails in government. In short, instead of observing a constant dialogue, we usually observe "rituals" represented by useless conversations.

How should you start a dialogue with those who consider themselves to be the main experts in a field in which you are now the leader?

I will share some thoughts on how to take advantage of some opportunities to promote a better dialogue between a Minister or Secretary of Education and the research community.

**Start off on the right foot.** Just like in many other communities, a newcomer will probably be examined in detail. There will be enthusiastic researchers and those frustrated by your recent appointment. Given the high turnover rate observed among Secretaries of Education, and the long periods that usually prevail in academia, be prepared to be examined by a community where members know each other well. Obviously you do not need to be "approved" by them (the approval needed to become Secretary or Minister has already been given to you by the President), but it is important to show the researchers a genuine desire to: a) know and learn; b) show interest in the available research; and c) listen to a community that, whether you like it or not, will always assume it knows more than you do about the sector that you are now leading.

**Trust.** Developing open spaces for dialogue will require researchers to trust the Secretary, and vice versa. Be clear – very clear– about what you intend to modify and achieve in your political term, give opportunity to question some of your proposals in a constructive way and, above all, recognize what has been done well by your predecessors. This is a strategy that will help create an environment of openness with the community of educational researchers.

**Openness.** The diversity of political positions, methodologies, and guiding principles adopted by researchers is as rich as the diversity of positions you will find in any political organization. Try to listen to members of different research communities, without becoming associated with any one in particular. A Secretary needs to learn from multiple perspectives.

**Promote disagreement.** Nothing discourages a researcher more than seeing a Secretary shaking his or her head when s/he hears a phrase that begins to question a decision already made. It is important to respect what researchers know, in the same way that it is important for you to always question what is *not* known, what is *not* scalable or feasible, or what has not been studied in the local context.

**Continuity.** A serious research community will not consider a single conversation to represent a real dialogue. If you want to develop a meaningful relationship with the research community, dialogue should be a constant activity. Obviously, these meetings may interfere with other multiple important meetings already included in your agenda, they may result in more meetings that reiterate discussions on issues that you already think you know well, and they may even distract you from urgent political issues. But it is important to maintain an open perspective to find points of mutual interest with scholars and, above all, to find new ideas or concepts that may result in innovations and improvements in your educational strategies and interventions, regardless of the goals you have set for both.

**Political ambitions.** If there is anything that drives a researcher away, it is a Secretary of Education who considers his/her post only as a temporary step for the next political position. You lose all credibility. Ensure that this perception does not prevail among researchers, at least if you want to find a community that will genuinely help you think about how to improve the education system.

**Develop networks**. A fruitful dialogue will probably start with participation of the Secretary, but dialogue must continue with the participation of his/her working group. It is impossible for the Secretary to lead and remain at the forefront of any initiative that emerges from the research community. It is necessary to generate networks with people from different institutions and from different areas within the Secretariat or Ministry. It will be the best way to prevent an innovation or project from being terminated too soon.

**Discern, accept or reject.** Not everything a researcher proposes will work, nor are all proposals rejected by a Secretary poor policy ideas. In any case, it is important that your own informed judgment and experience prevail. You should question what is suggested by scholars, but at the same time be open to criticisms towards your own decisions. This should not result in conflicts but rather be considered by both groups as opportunities to continue learning.

**Popularity does not always mean reliable and useful research**. In your dialogue and outreach, you should not only consider the most renowned or well-known researchers. There will be pleasant surprises if you approach younger or foreign scholars.

**Abundance does not mean relevance.** A necessary *mea culpa*: Every year, hundreds or thousands of publications will appear. However, there will be numerous questions that you will ask researchers for which they will not have a clear explanation. In other cases, the answer you will get will not help you to make a better decision. Furthermore, you will learn that despite countless papers and published articles, national researchers have not addressed some relevant topics yet. Regardless of the answers you may get, please remember that keeping an ongoing and healthy exchange with this community might be crucial to support your initiatives.

# Letter to a new Minister of Education

## Jaime Saavedra

*Jaime Saavedra leads the Education Global Practice at the World Bank Group. He rejoined the World Bank Group from the Government of Peru, where he served as Minister of Education from 2013 through 2016. During his tenure, the performance of Peru's education system improved substantially as measured by international learning assessments. He has held positions at a number of international organizations and think-tanks, among them the Inter-American Development Bank, the Economic Commission for Latin America and the Caribbean, the International Labour Organization, the Grupo de Análisis para el Desarollo, and the National Council of Labor in Peru. He has also held teaching and research positions in academia and has published extensively.*

You are embarking on what is probably the most important job you will ever have. If you don't realize that or if the country does not understand that the role of Minister of Education is one of the most critical public posts that might determine the long-run viability of the country, then maybe the country as a whole, the executive, the business elite, and the political leaders do not really understand the crucial role that education plays. Not only as a right, which it is, but also as the key determinant of growth, development and competitiveness. If there is no political alignment behind education, you will have to fight to position education so that these constituencies understand its importance. Education is about giving the right quality service to all children and youth, and as such, it is a long-run endeavor that requires the full political commitment of the executive, of parliament, and of society in general.

You have to fight to make sure that the macro financial complex, the executive, the business elite, the political leadership, public opinion, trade unions, media, teachers, parliament, local authorities, and parents understand that providing a decent education service to all is an inescapable precondition for having a viable economy and society. There must be political alignment around education reform so that student learning is always the sole focus of reform efforts. A system that is focused on learning sounds obvious, but it isn't. A high-performing education system that delivers learning for all requires a financial, managerial and political commitment from all those actors.

You will hear that education is a soft sector. That the hard investments are in roads, ports, housing, energy, or logistics. That is not true. There is nothing soft in a sector that is about providing a high-quality service for millions of students, working with hundreds of thousands or even millions of teachers and principals, in tens of thousands of establishments. Quality education is a service –or an experience– that is ultimately about making children and youth happy, self-confident, creative, curious, good citizens who are prepared for life and prepared for a world and future job market where the only certainty is uncertainty. An extremely difficult service to provide.

Even if quality education sounds like a commendable goal that everyone will be glad to align behind, at the same time it is a huge economic sector, and there are many interests and political forces, some positive and some negative, that make education reform extremely complex from an economic, financial and political perspective. This explains why education is always front and center in any politician's list of electoral promises, but once in office, in many cases, real education reform stalls.

Many times, interests other than student learning influence the behavior of different actors, and those include the interests of politicians who lobby to provide benefits to special groups. In fact, trade unions might seek political influence and political objectives. Bureaucrats might try to protect their power base or their jobs. Teachers might be fixated on job security, might be worried about being evaluated or about any pay-for-performance scheme. Service providers, meanwhile, in their quest for profit, might push for solutions that don't promote student welfare, or may be interested in providing well marketed but low-quality service. Suppliers of textbooks, suppliers of low-quality universities, providers of private tutoring services that support rote learning and hence prefer an evaluation system that values memorization – Egypt will be a typical case; all might be interested in maintaining the status quo, even if that means that children are not learning. These interests must be confronted head-on. If all these actors are happy and no one criticizes you, most likely you are not doing much or are not doing the right things. If for whatever reason someone told you that you could keep a technocratic profile, you will discover soon that to be a fantasy.

From a short-run economic perspective, education is a macro sector. In a typical middle-income country, education accounts for somewhere between 15% and 20% of the public budget – almost a fifth of the state. Teachers comprise the largest occupation within the public sector labor force. Changes in labor policies regarding teachers may have an impact on the whole labor market of teachers (even if the private market is not regulated) as the public sector is the largest buyer in the market of professionals in general. Teachers' salaries are a very significant portion of public expenditures. Aggregate demand can be influenced through the education sector as well. In the budgetary process, education is sometimes seen as consumption and not as an investment. That is clearly wrong. Education is investing in human capital, with exactly the same influence in productivity and competitiveness, and on potential GDP, as machines or roads. This is something that macroeconomists usually forget as soon as they take their final exam on growth theory during their PhDs.

The other side of the coin, the financing structure, is different. Probably this is the most significant difference between education and physical capital: that the expansion of the system and quality improvements of the education service that require changes in education expenditures, require *permanent* changes in fiscal revenues. You can invest in a bridge today, and if the macroeconomic cycle goes into a downturn, you can postpone the next bridge. In the case of the educational machinery, the expansion needed to make sure that everyone receives the adequate service is permanent, and hence requires permanent additional fiscal financing. That is why the discussion and the definition of the long-term educational objectives in a country require all of government and a high degree of social commitment. It is a central part of the social contract of the country.

You will be asked to prioritize: choose between technical education or early childhood education, choose between expanding a better service for children with disabilities or mother tongue education, etc. It is very difficult. There are very clear social and economic reasons why it is critical to invest in early childhood education in the same way as the case can be made for technical education. There are also reasons to provide a good service to children with disabilities and to make sure that all students are taught in their mother tongue during their first years of schooling. Most likely, you will have to tackle all fronts. But there will be a *de facto* prioritization because in practice it is difficult to tackle all issues at once. Even large teams have a limited band-width. Some issues might be more urgent than others, some will have a clear political window, others will require more political work and analysis. It is critical though, to set a very high level of ambition. There is probably no country where the task in education is to just make some marginal changes and keep the machinery working. In most cases, and in particular in all middle- and low-income countries, the ambition has to be high. In most cases, permanent and sustained structural reform is needed. In some cases that reform must be started, in others (the minority, unfortunately) reforms are already ongoing and momentum must be sustained.

You need to capture the imagination of the people. People need to see and believe that things are moving. I have seen many countries' education sector plans. The good ones are comprehensive and provide a reasonably complete roadmap. But that is not enough. They have to be short, useful, and understandable by people from all disciplines, including by journalists and opinion makers. Or at least there has to be a version of the document that has those characteristics. And the plan must define milestones that are attainable (and visible) in the short or medium term, as well as long-term goals.

Leadership is critical. You must own the reform and be the cheerleader-in-chief. Give a sense of mission to all people who work in the Ministry and in schools. Everyone must recognize that her job has a direct and profound impact on whether students learn, which is the ultimate objective of their work. Pedagogical experts should ensure a pragmatic, realistic curriculum that clearly defines the skills students should acquire throughout the schooling process. The curriculum must constitute an effective and useful guide for teachers (and not become an incomprehensible phone book that nobody uses, as you still see in some Latin American countries). Administrators need to ensure that the inputs needed for effective learning (from the textbook, the lesson plan and the chalkboad, to the tablet and the software that helps students learn at their own pace) are all there, on time, and available to all schools and students.

Teachers must internalize that their job is not to passively teach, but to actively make sure that every student in the classroom learns (which is the case among the high-performing systems in East Asia). And for the magic of learning to happen, teachers must be selected meritocratically and receive constant training, guidance, and feedback throughout their careers. Principals should be selected and trained to be managers of a complex institution that is the school, but they should also be pedagogical and institutional leaders who manage and inspire their workforce, with the end goal of making sure all students in the school learn. There are many countries who do not pay attention to the career of the principal, which is a big mistake.

But being the education leader also comes with the responsibility of maintaining a focus on reality. People must know where the country stands. Education is an extremely complex sector, and in most low- and middle-income countries, the needs and gaps will be immense. It is politically tempting to try to emphasize the progress, the improvements, and the short-run victories. That is tempting and human. And it is also needed. But that must be balanced with a dose of reality.

Just three weeks after becoming Minister of Education in Peru, we received the results from the 2012 round of PISA.

Peru was ranked last. Not next to last, not bottom 10%. It was last. Education, which never made headlines, was on the front page of the main Peruvian newspaper. For the local media, the fact that PISA is only administered to a subset of countries was not important, that was just a footnote. For the media, Peruvian students were the worst in the world.

We could have tried to explain this away by identifying countries that would have ranked worse than Peru if they had participated (almost all low-income countries and many middle-income ones). Or we could have accused the PISA initiative of being a "rich country" endeavour with little relevance to the culture or national priorities of Peru. Or we could have tried to give relevance to the fact that Peru had improved in its scores (although other countries improved more, hence it fell in the ranking). An even worse reaction could have been to withdraw from PISA as a few other countries have done after receiving bad news.

Instead, the Peruvian government recognized that the PISA results revealed that we had a huge learning challenge. That despite past progress, we had not invested enough in education. That the efficiency of educational expenditures had to improve. And that we all had to work together to fix it. The country embarked on a reform that built on the progress of previous efforts and looked to accelerate improvements in learning.

Education became a topic that everyone—from taxi drivers to politicians from all parties—talked about. The assessment, and the understanding that the country was far from where it should be, created social and political consensus in Peru to dramatically increase spending for education, and implement major reforms that otherwise would have been very difficult.

Resistance to reforms might originate in very entrenched interests of specific stakeholders. Reform is usually extremely challenging politically, and in countries with very large gaps, there is a sense of inevitability around the status quo. Hence governments might be tempted to just tinker around the edges without really tackling the real impediments to reform. I personally witnessed that in my own country. For a time, public perception was that education, and in particular public education, which serves 75% of the population, was and would forever be of bad quality because it was impossible to reform and it was impossible to move the system to deliver good quality. That teachers were not well qualified, were not interested in children's learning, were only interested in keeping their jobs, and would oppose to any attempt at reform. Time proved that wrong. Change is possible.

Change only starts to happen when the system puts politics and special interests aside and focuses on learning. This is the needed political alignment which has happened in the Scandinavian countries and in some of the East Asian countries. This is what happened in Sobral, in Ceara, a poor district in the north of Brazil which in about a decade moved to the top of the Brazilian education quality index. There, the mayor explained that one of the key elements for the successful learning reform was to reach the political consensus to leave politics out of the classroom.

Political alignment is critical. Everyone has to be convinced about the importance that investing in people has in the future of the country. And that understanding has to go well beyond the rhetoric. Teachers must be convinced of the importance of making the needed changes to improve the quality of education. And they must be convinced of the importance of their own role. Businesses and families must be convinced of the importance of education for the future of their families and the country; very pragmatically, better education in most cases will require more resources, and those will eventually come from the taxes that they will have to pay. The amount of taxes that will go –or should go– to finance education will be very significant. The political alignment should be forged around a reasonable policy design. I say "reasonable" because a perfectly designed policy does not exist. You need to design policies that incentivize the right behavior from all actors (teachers, principals, administrators and managers), and that provide the right support for all of them to be able to perform adequately. This design must be paired with a mechanism to assess if implementation is following the right course, to identify and measure impact, and to improve the policy over time.

And that design should be conceived at the scale needed to provide quality education to all. Your responsibility are ALL children and youth. Many education interventions that are supported by NGOs, foundations, international organizations, or the Ministry itself, have a certain budget and define their actions according to what they can finance. Many countries see education spending as implementing programs or partial improvements that will cover a group of teachers or schools, according to budget availability. That is fine as long as it is part of a plan that has as the ultimate objective to provide quality service to *all* children and youth. The full implementation of that plan may take 8 or 10 years, but reaching *all* students must be the planned outcome.

And the other key element to drive change is implementation capacity. This is also related to political commitment. It is not by chance that the most effective and better trained bureaucracies are always in Ministries of Finance or Central Banks. Implementation capacity varies among civil services in different countries and contexts. In many cases, it is the main obstacle to the success of policy change. A country's ability to execute change depends largely on the quality of its civil service, as well as on the organizational and incentive structures of the Ministries. As a result, countries need civil servants in the education sector who have adequate technical and management know-how, as well as commitment and a clear understanding of the importance of their mandate. If there is a clear understanding that education is a critical task, there will be a concerted and collective effort to shore-up the quality and commitment of education bureaucracies. When these three factors come together –reasonable design, implementation capacity, and political alignment– student learning can improve dramatically.

You will have a chance to affect many people's lives, more than in many other critical and valuable public sector jobs. You can start a reform or continue one, in the area that is probably the sole most important determinant of the future of your nation.

# Education System Reforms in Poland: What can be Learned from Past Mistakes?

## Przemysław Sadura and Jerzy Wiśniewski

*Przemysław Sadura, Ph.D. DSc, sociologist, publicist and translator. He is an assistant professor at the Institute of Sociology, University of Warsaw, and from Jan 2019 to Feb 2020 Visiting scholar at University College London School of Slavonic and East European Studies (SSEES). His fields of interest include relations between the state and class structure, citizen participation, public services and education. He has been engaged as a Principal Investigator or Main Contractor/Researcher in several dozen research projects for various institutions, including the European Research Council, the Polish National Science Centre, and the Polish Ministry of Regional Development. His most important current projects include: 1) 2019-2020 – SSEES UCL Class differences in Polish immigrants attitudes toward education and public institutions in the UK, research project Position Principal Investigator; 2) 2015-2019 Leiden University/ERC European Research Council Democratic Secrecy: A Philosophical Study of the Role of Secrecy in Democratic Governance Position: researcher; and 3) 2017-2019 University of Wroclaw/NCN "Social Structure, Social Networks and Consumer Tastes and Practices". Position: Main contractor. He is author or co-author of several books and dozens of articles.*

*Jerzy Wiśniewski is an expert on education policy. He started his professional career as a teacher of mathematics in Poland. In 1990, he joined the Ministry of National Education and headed several departments of the Ministry being responsible for strategy planning, international co-operation and coordination of the European Social Fund intervention in the educational sector in Poland. He served as Director General of the Ministry in 1998 as an overall system reform of Polish education was launched. He was instrumental in initiating the participation of Poland in OECD studies and programs such as INES, PISA, TALIS and PIAAC, as well as IEA programs PIRLS and TIMSS. Jerzy contributed to the OECD review of education in Lithuania and led the European Training Foundation team reviewing the VET system in Croatia. He has also led international research projects, including* Cross-curricular key competences and teacher education, *a study covering 27 EU Member States, and* The application of the learning outcome approach across Europe – a comparative perspective. *He was a member of OECD Centre for Educational Research and Innovation, European Commission High Level Group of experts on literacy (2011-12), the Selection Committee for WISE Prize in Education 2011 and the European Training Foundation Governing Board. Jerzy is the Vice-chair of the Board of the European Institute of Education and Social Policy, and a member of the Board of Education for the Democracy Foundation.*

## Introduction

According to Neville Bennett[13] it is as difficult to change the education system as it is to put a man on the Moon. Yet, astronauts have already walked on the Silver Globe and education reforms have been successfully accomplished in some countries. Why is this not the case in Poland? A great

---

[13] Bennett, Neville. (1976), *Teaching Styles and Pupil Progress*, London: Open Book.

number of changes have been made in Polish schools but, unlike the Apollo program, continuity and consistency were not trademarks of their implementation.

The last 50 years have seen a great number of changes introduced in the Polish education system. Most of them had a promising start but were ultimately abandoned due to opposition and resistance from various groups. Election cycles often gave a newly elected political party the pretext to launch a new reform initiative while ignoring previous efforts, both the achievements and the mistakes. That inefficient, repetitive pattern of preparing and implementing changes in education seems to be the rule in Poland.

Below, we focus on the biggest reform of the education system, introduced in 1999, and consider what can be learned from that experience.

**The Reform of 1999: Context and Objectives**

The profound changes in Central Europe, which began in 1989 in Poland, centered on the change from a centralized Soviet-style governance and economic system, to a liberal democracy and market economy. One could expect that education reform would quickly follow; however, for a decade, no such efforts were undertaken due to popular belief about the high quality of Polish education. Moreover, policymakers, who were advised by researchers, considered that 'no revolution is good for education.'

Finally, in 1997, the newly formed government decided to launch a comprehensive reform of the whole education system. It was part of the government's 'program of four reforms,' which included also reforms of the social security system (pensions), public administration and healthcare.

The objectives for the reform in education were to:

- Raise educational attainment by increasing the number of graduates of upper secondary and tertiary education programs;

- Ensure equal educational opportunities;

- Enhance the quality of education.

To achieve these objectives, the Ministry of Education changed the structure of the school system, redesigned curricula, and introduced external student assessment. The change of the structure of the system was a pivotal part of the reform as well as the most 'visible.' The previous structure had two-levels: an 8-year primary school and 3 to 5 years of secondary education. This was replaced with a three-level system, which included a 6-year primary school, a 3-year comprehensive lower secondary school, and 3-4 years of upper secondary education (vocational or general). In effect, these changes meant that a general, comprehensive education, which would introduce all young people to the same curriculum, was extended by one year and so the selection for various types of general and vocational upper secondary schools was also postponed by one year. The new lower secondary schools were to raise the quality of education particularly in rural areas. With bigger catchment areas, those schools would be large enough to provide teaching hours for teachers with subject specialization.

The structural change of the school system was a prerequisite for changes to the curriculum, on which the success of the overall reform depended. Detailed, centralized regulations were replaced by a national core curriculum. Teachers and schools would be responsible for their own decisions about the syllabus, textbooks and methods. Granting teachers greater autonomy was accompanied by the introduction of external standardized exams that would be taken by all students at the end of their primary and lower secondary education. The final secondary school exam (*matura*) replaced the entrance exams to higher education institutions. Although not obligatory, all students aspiring to a higher education took the *matura*.

**The Pros and Cons of the 1999 Reform**

The reform was introduced very quickly between the end of 1997, when the first concept of the reform was presented, and September 1999, when new lower secondary schools admitted the first cohort of students. Initially, opposition to the reform was limited. Criticism grew soon after the implementation of the reform. A significant reason was that reorganizing the school network and opening new schools was a challenge for local governments who were uncertain whether a new per-capita formula used for calculating their funds would ensure sufficient resources. Problems arose also in villages where primary schools, shortened to six years by the reform, became too small to survive. People in rural regions remembered similar reforms introduced in the 1970s, which aimed to improve the quality of education by closing small (and expensive) local schools and developing the network of larger municipal schools. Lack of understanding about the reform objectives, poor performance by the new schools, and problems with transportation to schools caused strong social resistance, which turned the reform project into a fiasco.

The 1999 reform followed the same trajectory as reform efforts in the 1970s in that there was practically no public consultation. Interestingly, the greatest opposition to the reform in 1999 was observed in those communities that were the most active during the 1970s protests. The government did not recognize the emotional attachment that residents felt to local schools and also ignored the importance of collective social memory as a foundation for resistance. Citizens, who did not trust the state, assumed that the local government would not provide children with transportation and the schools with adequate staff and equipment.

Attitudes among teachers towards the reform were varied. Some saw the opening of new schools and their greater autonomy as an opportunity to promote innovative approaches to teaching and learning and to experiment with new teaching methods. These teachers were positive about the changes. Still, a large group of teachers were reluctant to support the reform. These included teachers who were concerned about implementing the new curriculum and anxious about their students' results on the new external exams. Teachers in upper secondary schools complained that they had less time (three years instead of four) to go through the curriculum in order to prepare students for the external high-stakes final exam.

Moreover, the new lower secondary schools faced behavioral problems typical of young teenagers. These negative experiences have remained in the collective memory and continue to mark public opinion, even though by now teachers have developed methods to address the problems and to work effectively with teenage students.

Negative public opinion should be confronted with evidence-based evaluations of the education reforms, even if such evaluations can be a challenge to carry out. Poland was lucky to benefit from the first PISA (Programme for International Student Assessment) study to evaluate the 1999 reform. The study was first carried out in 2000. At that time, 15-year-old students (the age group targeted by PISA) were not affected by the structural reform. The second cycle of PISA, in 2003, included students who were in the final grade of the new lower secondary schools. This means that the group targeted by PISA 2000 can serve as a benchmark against which to 'evaluate' the impact of the reform in consecutive cycles of the study.

Such an 'evaluation'[14] gives very positive results. Poland improved its scores significantly in all domains. In the reading test, average student achievement of students was 479 in the year 2000, increasing to 497 in the year 2003 and to 508 in 2006.

Moreover, an analysis[15] of the distribution of students' learning outcomes revealed an increase in average results between 2000 and 2003. This improvement was due mostly to a reduced number of low achievers and to significant progress among students who, in the old system, would have ended up in vocational schools.

The continued improvement of PISA results among Polish students (in 2012, the score was 518 in reading and math, and 526 in science, all significantly above the OECD average) has not, however, helped to change the popular view that Polish schools offer poor quality education. In public opinion polls, 50% of respondents support the elimination of lower

---

[14] We don't see PISA as an evaluation of the education reform in the strict sense. The PISA study did not take all relevant factors into account and, indeed, it was not designed to be an 'evaluation' of the reform. It can, however, serve as a partial evaluation of some aspects of the reform.

[15] Jakubowski, M., Patrinos, H., Port, E, and Wisniewski, J. (2016), *The effects of delaying tracking in secondary school: evidence from the 1999 education reform in Poland*. Education Economics, 1–16. doi: 10.1080/09645292.2016.1149548

secondary schools, which are perceived as the most problematic element of the post-reform system.[16]

## New Reforms, Old Problems

There were also other problems that emerged after the reform. In large cities, lower secondary schools started to play with the rules that were set for catchment areas and introduced solutions that, in practice, amounted to selection in the recruitment processes. The Ministry did not oppose such practices. In effect, differences grew between lower secondary schools in terms of the socio-demographic profile of the student body and students' education results. Middle class students concentrated in the best schools and less privileged children remained in the rest.[17] The government did not combat these symptoms of segregation in schools and, instead, attempted to reduce inequalities in access to education in other ways. In 2008 the government lowered the school starting age (from seven to six), which was supposed to increase access to kindergartens, especially among children from families of lower socioeconomic status. Parents in the middle class perceived this change as unnecessary, while working class parents were not aware of

---

[16] For more on the 1999 reform in a comparative perspective see: Herbst, M., and A. Wojciuk. (2014), "Common Origin, Different Paths. Transformation of Education Systems in the Czech Republic, Slovakia, Hungary and Poland," GRINCOH Working Paper, Warsaw: University of Warsaw Press.

[17] Dolata, R. (2013), *Międzyszkolne zróżnicowanie wyników nauczania na poziomie szkoły podstawowej i gimnazjum. Raport podsumowujący,* Warszawa: Instytut Badań Edukacyjnych.

the benefits. The government did not address such opinions or lack of information. When a public survey on reform was finally carried out, it showed that people from both groups –over 80% of respondents– were against the change, although for different reasons. This general dissatisfaction produced a national movement to "Save the toddlers".

In the 2015 election campaign, the then-opposition party appealed to a general nostalgia for the "good old times" and capitalized on the negative opinions of the school reform. They promised, among other populist proposals, to reverse the education reform by bringing back the old structure of the education system (thus eliminating lower secondary schools) and raising the school starting age to seven. When the party won the election, they quickly pushed new regulations through Parliament and reversed the reforms.

This brief analysis presented above shows that actions taken by the Polish government were characterized by management through legislation and top-down control, as well as inconsistency and low responsiveness to public opinion.[18] Goodwill on the part of reformers is not sufficient.

---

[18] For more on these issues, see: Kordasiewicz A., Sadura P. (2017), *Clash of Public Administration Paradigms in Delegation of Education and Elderly Care Services in a Post-socialist State (Poland)* "Public Management Review" Vol. 19 , Issue 6, pp.: 785-801. Online: http://www.tandfonline.com/doi/full/10.1080/14719037.2016.1210 903.

Effective public relations and communication are necessary for reforms to be successful. The reforms discussed above were not preceded by public consultations nor accompanied by reliable public information campaigns. No effort was made to build broad public support for the planned changes. No potential "unintended consequences of reforms" were identified or addressed. Furthermore, poor monitoring of reform implementation made it difficult to react adequately and quickly when public opinion turned negative. Inconsistency in introducing changes undermined the already low trust in the state and public institutions. Patronizing attitudes meant that changes were implemented 'for' and not 'with' the people. For these reasons, so many potential beneficiaries of the reforms ultimately turned against them.

**What next?**

The conclusions that can be drawn from this brief analysis can be summarized in the following list of recommendations for successful reform in education:

- A rigorous and detailed diagnosis and impact assessment that is evidence-based and takes into account both the positive and the negative experiences of previously implemented reforms is a crucial foundation.

- Public consultations are needed at the design stage as well as during the implementation of reforms, as they also have a crucial monitoring function. Consultations should not be treated as a tool for manipulating public opinion. The voice of minority groups, including those with lower socioeconomic status, should be empowered.

- Information about the reform's objectives should be broadly disseminated within the frame of a professional communication strategy. The content and dissemination channels should be sensitive and adapted to specific social groups (e.g. socioeconomic status, gender, age, ethnic background, etc.).

- Take the politics out of education. It is crucial to break the vicious circle of adjusting reform initiatives to election cycles. Nonpartisan initiatives, civic organizations and the media should have a strong role in building broad social support for reform projects.

- Persistence is key in reform implementation. Any change in reform objectives and in the implementation process should be openly communicated, clearly explained, and backed up by concrete data, evidence and analysis.

# Letter to a young minister: A few things I wish I knew when I came to office
## Nuno Crato

*Nuno Crato is Professor of Mathematics and Statistics at the University of Lisbon. For many years he has been concerned with education, science, and cultural issues, publishing a few books and receiving awards for his writings. From 2011 to 2015 he was Minister of Education and Science in Portugal. During his tenure, mandatory schooling was extended from 9 to 12 grades, English was introduced as a mandatory discipline for seven consecutive school years, additional resources were directed to fundamental disciplines and to elementary education, new vocational paths were developed, and dropout rates were reduced from approximately 25% to 13.7%. In 2015, Portugal obtained its best results to date in international assessments: for the first time the country surpassed the OECD average in PISA and 4th graders obtained a remarkable result in TIMSS, surpassing Finish students' results.*

A few months after becoming Minister, I started saying that "no one who has never before been an Education Minister should ever become an Education Minister". This silly joke wasn't usually understood. But what I meant was clear to me: this is the type of job for which we are always unprepared.

How can someone who has the advantage of having had such an experience be useful to those who are initiating it?

Maybe I can do so by listing a few recommendations that at least for me proved to be more important than I had expected.

## 1.  Do no harm!

Unfortunately, many Ministers come to the job without a clear plan. They are appointed for political reasons, to fill a post or fulfill an ambition. Some don't have any experience in education, just general political convictions unrelated to educational issues. Many times, during my four-year-and-some-months tenure, I met new Ministers of Education who candidly confessed to be novices, just trying to understand their job. In the European Council of Education Ministers, which met almost every other month, I found many new ministers eager to learn from their colleagues. At other international venues, such as the OECD or the Iberian-American meetings, I found colleagues with similar concerns.

Disappointingly, a few weeks later those same Ministers who started their job very humbly and cautiously, had many definite and revolutionary ideas for education.

My advice for such cases may seem a bit arrogant: *either quit or try to do no harm*. Education is a very serious and particular issue, and it's very easy to be convinced of some radical ideas and pursue them without any caution. To make things worse, everybody –literally everybody– acts as if they had definitive ideas on education, and supposedly good, righteous ones.

This is a puzzle to me to this day: how is it possible that so many people, including some considered educational experts, have so many nonsensical ideas and are so convinced of being right without any consideration of the rich, extensive, controversial, and complicated history of education and education research?

An education system is a system... by this I mean that an education system is a complex network with interacting mechanisms and we cannot improve the general results just by tinkering with one component and disregarding its interaction with the other components. Sometimes, for instance, some Ministers have tried to introduce more freedom in the system by giving more autonomy to schools and abandoning all types of testing and supervision. Sometimes, the ensuing results have been regretful: schools and teachers were not prepared and had no idea how to manage a less defined curriculum, and students' results plunged. Other times, education authorities have thought that computers would modernize schools and entice students to learn. Nothing wrong with this idea, but computers can be distracting and useless tools if there are no computer learning applications and if teachers and students have no idea how to use them in classrooms for instructional purposes. A few countries had disastrous and expensive experiences in this regard.

So, if I may give you some advice, I'd say: don't invent if you are not sure of what you are doing, always question your beliefs, *do no harm,* manage the Ministry, try to solve the most pressing issues, and try to establish a dialogue with your partners –teachers, principals, parents, unions– but don't be a slave to any of them. Visit schools, encourage students, encourage parents, dignify education. If you succeed in these apparently simple tasks, be confident that you have already become an excellent Minister. If you try to learn and do one or two things well, improving education just a bit, you have been an outstanding Minister.

## 2.   Don't believe the experts.

The moment you become Minister, you will find new best friends everywhere. People whom you forgot existed will approach you with wonderful suggestions. Friends who haven't called you in ages will congratulate you and –by the way– ask you for a job for some very qualified but underappreciated relative. Very honest people who criticize all politicians as corrupt will approach you asking for a favour that is simply unfair and discriminatory to other people. And they will naturally criticize you if you don't bend to their requests.

Worse of all are people who will encircle you because they have forever been at the Ministry as highly-ranked officers and permanent advisers, or because they have always had business and partnerships with the Ministry. These people never criticize you, and suddenly and naturally discover you are a much better person than your political competitors or your predecessors. They are experts in seduction. You can't rival their experience. You can't outsmart them. But you must contain them. And you can't do without them.

You need people who have been at the Ministry, who know the system. But you will soon realize that some of them have different views. Always hear them. Always hear both sides. Try to think for yourself and keep hearing criticisms.

This is difficult. However, if you are cautious, you will achieve no daring goals, but will avoid costly mistakes.

## 3. Pay attention to data.

When you start your work, you may not be aware of the importance of many simple but decisive statistics. You may be interested in improving the curriculum but pay no attention to dropout rates; you may be interested in improving school facilities but forget about curricular outcomes; you may be interested in improving teachers' salaries but forget about student retention.

When you approach your second year in office you start realizing the crucial importance of some basic statistics. They mean a lot to the education system and you are going to be judged by them.

Are student grade completion rates increasing? Are student dropout rates decreasing? Are students performing reasonably in PISA, TIMSS and similar assessments? Are school bullying and school violence occurrences being reduced? Are there more students finishing high school and enrolling in post-secondary and tertiary college programs? At the same time, is the average number of students per class reasonable? Is the student-per-teacher ratio reasonable? Are general expenses appropriately contained?

To pay attention to data doesn't mean you should tinker with data, fiddle with them, or pressure statistical authorities to change results. It means two things: first, to make sure data are coherently and consistently presented, that some officer doesn't decide to suddenly alter criteria in such a way that results look much different; second, that you should pay attention to individual policy changes that are going to affect data results and the evolution of the main indicators. Indicators are just that: indicators – they don't represent the whole reality. But often they mean a lot, they may mean more than what you think, and bad results are costly.

**4. Choose to be a Minister of students' future.**

This is my final and maybe more important advice. If you are a Minister of Education your main duty is with the nation: with students' education and training, and students' future. However, those are not the most vocal voices in education. Unions, parents, civil servants, political parties and pressure groups are much more active, much better heard, and much better amplified by the media.

If you have teachers' unions fighting for better salaries and a shorter working schedule, be sure the slogans will be noble: we need "to dignify the teaching profession", schools and teachers need time to "prepare their classes and to contact students", or teachers need "opportunities to help students become active citizens". All these noble slogans may be true in a substantial sense. But you must judge: are teachers truly badly paid, as is the case in many countries?

Will the reduction in allocation of class hours be used in favour of students' preparation?

I'd bet that 90% of the times 90% of the claims, although perhaps fair, are not about students. Yet, students should be your major concern. It's easy to be fooled, and your duty is to think about those who are not voicing their opinion.

\* \* \*

If you think you have just wasted your time reading this simple list of recommendations, maybe you will find time for us to talk again when you leave office. I wish you the best. Better yet: I wish your country's youth the best!

### References

*Learning to Lead: Four Principles for Ministers of Education to Survive and Succeed in Government,* The Varkey Foundation, 2018. Accessed in September 2018 https://www.varkeyfoundation.org/media/4228/learning-to-lead-four-principles-for-ministers-april-2018-1ps.pdf.

Michael Barber, *How to Deliver Improved Outcomes for School Systems,* The WISE Foundation, 2017. Accessed in September 2018 https://www.wise-qatar.org/sites/default/files/rr.4.2017_barber.pdf.

# Lessons from Reform in Russia

## (2001—2017)

## Isak Froumin and Igor Remorenko

*Isak Froumin is the Head of the Institute of Education at the National Research University "Higher School of Economics" in Moscow (Russia), the first graduate school of education in Russia. Prof. Froumin led the World Bank's education program in Russia from 1999 to 2011. His World Bank experience also extends to projects in Kazakhstan, Kyrgyzstan, Afghanistan, Nepal, Turkmenistan, and India. From 2012 to 2016, he was an advisor to the Minister of Education and Science of the Russian Federation. Prof. Froumin is an editor and author of more than 250 publications including articles and books in Russian and English.*

*Dr. Igor M. Remorenko has been holding the post of Rector of the Moscow City University (MCU) since 2013. From 2009 to 2011, he was Director of the Department of the National School Policy of the Ministry of Education and Science of the Russian Federation. He supervised the national project "Education". From 2011 to 2013, Dr. Remorenko was Deputy Minister of Education and Science of the Russian Federation. He was responsible for school-level education in the country.*

## Context

Within the first decade following the dissolution of the Soviet Union, the education system faced multiple critical challenges due to serious systemic and economic crises undermining all sectors of the economy and the whole social sphere more generally, which included significant budget cuts, wage reductions, the fall in prestige of the teaching profession, qualified professionals leaving the sphere, and equipment obsolescence (Bolotov and Lenskaya 1997; Scweisfurth 2002).

Since the early 2000s, Russia started a new phase of education reforms, no longer a reactive approach to emerging needs and circumstances but rather an attempt to build an education system that will ensure the accelerated socio-economic development of the country.

Concurrently, by the beginning of 2001, a certain consensus had developed in the expert community in Russia on the kind of changes which would help improve the education system, which found expression in a *Concept note on Modernization of Russian Education by the Year of 2010* that was issued in 2001 and which contained the following ideas:

- The creation of an independent system of education quality assessment, including the creation and improvement of the procedures for independent nationwide standardized final school examinations;
- Improvement of the structure of school education, making the transition to vocational schools and universities more flexible;
- Development of a modern educational environment, partly due to computerization and provision of access to the Internet, as well as development of digital educational resources for all levels and stages of education;
- Implementation of per-capita financing; and

- The transformation of the system of education governance based on the principle of the division of responsibilities between federal, regional and municipal governing bodies and educational institutions, and on real public involvement in the decision-making process (Concept for Modernisation 2010).

However, actual implementation of these ideas would take more time. The "vigor" of the state was first rendered in a form of support for improvements to infrastructure and changes in education leaders — "points of growth." In 2005, the President of the Russian Federation Vladimir Putin decided to make more focused efforts, and he declared four national projects of priority, among which there was the National Priority Project "Education" (NPPE).

The main actions of the NPPE in the sphere of school education that were launched in 2006 were the following:

- The provision of connection of schools to the Internet;
- The provision of school buses for rural areas;
- The provision of modern equipment to schools; and
- The provision of development grants for best schools.

One can see that these actions focused on inputs and on resources, and not on institutional reforms. The *institutional changes* listed in the Concept of Modernization of Education would only start to take place in 2007. They appeared in the framework of complex project of education system modernization on a regional level (CPME) (Compleksnyye proecty modernizatsii obrazovanya 2007):

- The implementation of a new system of remuneration of (NSRL) for teachers, which was intended to increase teachers' income;
- The transition to a normative per capita financing (NPCF) for schools, which meant that the volume of financing is calculated in relation to the number of students and the normative cost has to be set for the education of one person;
- The establishment of specialized education assessment organizations;
- The restructuring of the regional networks of schools (particularly in rural areas) to create bigger schools with better facilities; and
- The increase of public participation in education governances through the creation of managing and supervisory school boards in which pupils' parents could become members.

Thirty-one subjects of the Russian Federation (from 83) participated in the project in the pilot state.

The main principles of the implementation of this project (CPME) were: using a project approach (including the creation of an office of the project, the development of indicators for control and a system for monitoring their achievement, and clear timetable for project implementation); "money to incentivize reform" (the allocation of funds from the federal budget to regions in exchange for launching the reforms); and "money in return for results" (establishing a connection between the continuation of funds from the federal budget to regions if performance targets were achieved). It is worth pointing out that there were cases of administrative pressure.

A nation-wide school leaving exam –the *Unified State Exam* (USE)– was launched together with the CPME, first in a form of beta-testing, and later, starting from 2009, as a regular practice. The USE was designed to have two functions: as a final school assessment and as an entrance examination for higher education institutions. It was designed as a standardized high-stakes assessment.

The implementation of the USE significantly increased mobility school graduates across regions, increasing accessibility to quality higher education. For instance, the share of first year students in higher education institutions of Moscow increased more than twofold. On the other hand, it bred practices of drilling in educational process which became necessary to get students prepared and which decreased their overall level of cultural development. This decreased families' trust that schools were preparing students effectively for the USE, and as a result many started to resort to private tutors more and more frequently, which increased inequality.

An "educational" component of the described reforms was significantly less vigorously pushed than their "financial" and "administrative" components, at least during the first five years of it (2007—2010).

In an attempt to return to an initial "educational focus" of changes and to involve school principals and teachers into reform, President Medvedev issued a document called the

Presidential Initiative "Our New School." This initiative outlined the following key directions for the development of general education:

- The transition to new educational (curriculum) standards;
- The development of the system of support for gifted children;
- Teachers' professional development;
- The preservation and improvement of pupils' health in school setting; and
- Increasing school autonomy.

For the first time in Russia, regulation of the education content and the learning process became results-oriented rather than process-oriented (focusing of what it is necessary to "cover"). Many schools and teachers were involved in experiments and innovations within this initiative.

The experience of the implementation of the complex project (CPME) and "Our New School Initiative" provided the ground for the reform of the national education legal framework. New Federal Law No. 273 "On Education in the Russian Federation" was passed in 2012. This law made the organizational structure of education more flexible, set new forms of implementation of education programs, including family-based, and online. It broadened the scope of the rights of students and of their legal representatives (in most cases, parents), for instance, in terms of acquiring information about educational institutions and participating in the governing of an educational institution. For the first time in the history of Russia, the law covered the education rights to accommodation of individuals with disabilities. One of the main provisions was that the salary of a teacher could not be lower than the average salary for the considered region. All of the instruments of budgeting outlined earlier in his reflection received legislative status.

**Outcomes**

The education reforms of 2007—2017 in Russia should be assessed relative to the aims that were set forth for them.

Today, Russia holds strong positions in terms of coverage of school-aged children. Accessibility of school education is ensured across the whole country, even in its most distant corners and within conditions of severe climate and complicated demography. School infrastructure has been significantly improved both in terms of basic conditions (water supply, central heating, and drainage) as well as modern technologies (Internet access, computers, and other technical equipment).

Pupils finishing primary school demonstrate high levels of reading literacy in the a cross-national Progress in International Reading Literacy Study (PIRLS). In 2016, Russia became a leader among participating countries. Although this result was made possible mainly because of the contribution of families (through home reading practice), there is some evidence of the positive impact of the new education standards.

According to the data of the Trends in Mathematics and Science Study (TIMSS) of 2015, Russian pupils in the 4th and in the 8th year of education reached no lower than the 7th place in all subjects across all participating countries. Moreover, results of Russian students in TIMSS significantly improved from 2003, the year Russia first participated in the study.

Similarly, Russian students improved relative to other countries since 2003 in the Programme for International Student Assessment (PISA). In 2015, results of Russian pupils in reading and mathematics literacy were higher than the average results for the OECD countries, arguably an indication of the impact of the new education standards.

It is fair to say that the institutional reforms of Russian schools have been implemented. There are now conceptually new mechanisms of state regulation and funding, quality assessment, and education standards.

### Reflections

Within the last ten years, Russia has managed to transform the system of school education drastically. These changes have been comprehensive and broad-reaching. There is no doubt there were certain *deficits* in terms of the design of reforms and in their implementation.

First of all, it is important to mention the lack of consistency of the reforms. The measures that were implemented found their practical realization in quite a nonsynchronous and non-complementary way, often in an erratic order of steps.

As an example, we can look at policies related to teachers. The new system of wage calculation was put into practice long before the creation of a system for teaching quality assurance and assessment or the development of a professional standard. Similarly, the Unified State Examination was implemented prior to new education standards, and contradicts the new ideas about key competencies that are in the center of new standards.

At all times, reforms were carried out in a top-down and centralized manner, without due respect for the views of teachers and families, and without sufficient flexibility to adapt to regional specificities (even though it is commonly understood that Russia is a country with a high level of social, cultural, and economic heterogeneity).

The necessity of gaining the support of the reform's main stakeholders and beneficiaries (mainly teachers) was underestimated. There were almost no attempts to take steps in the direction of creating demand for the offered innovations and for the institutions that were being built. This was very distinctly seen, for instance, in the process of implementation of the new standards of education. Even in the situations in which reform measures obviously offered benefit and improvement, there was no ensured "leadership from the inside" and there was no effort to 'sell' the reform. Moreover, no feedback in terms of the results of changes was collected and taken into consideration, even though there obviously existed certain achievements (including the achievements proven by cross-national education quality assessment initiatives).

Often this attitude led to a "formal" approach to implementing changes and even their imitation. Instead of giving feedback in reports, schools often provided "glossy" bureaucratic papers designed no more than to show superficial compliance. To ensure the professionalism of teaching bodies, the emphasis was on creating personal incentives instead of developing the social capital of the system through the interactions of schools and teachers.

The principle of autonomy and independence was considered a linchpin in a new Russian school. However, in many ways it became a chink in the armor, which was explained earlier in discussing the education standards. The practice of granting sudden freedom without explaining and cultivating its importance and potential, put most specialists in the field in a very challenging position.

There are reasons to believe that, in a way, the effectiveness of the reforms was *limited* by the state's approach to education budgeting and allocation of funds.

At last, the system of allocation of responsibilities in education management and financing had a negative impact on the effectiveness of the reforms. According to the law "On Education in the Russian Federation" of 1992, responsibility for the provision of general education is divided between the federal center, the subjects of the country, and the municipalities. The federal center was to be responsible for the policy and to develop standards, and in some cases (the examples which were given) to use the tool of project management and financing. At the same time, the municipalities were to take the role of school holders making key decisions (on human resources, structural reorganization, and liquidation) and holding responsibility for the state of infrastructure.

Such structure created obstacles for effective controlled changes since "signals" from above were often distorted on the way or even lost, so responsibility frames were very vague. The "center" did not have direct tools for control and consistently underestimated the differences among the educational contexts where these changes had to be implemented. As a result, the national government gave the provinces and municipalities autonomy for the realization of the reform's goals, but at the same time, did not trust them and created bureaucratic mechanisms of control that required a lot of time and power to answer to. The same mechanism was automatically reproduced in terms of the relations between regional governing bodies and municipalities. Therefore, the legislatively set principle of autonomy found an extremely limited implementation capacity in practice.

Moreover, aspects of financial and managing capacity at the municipal level proved to be the weakest link. Conditions of infrastructure and labor remuneration varied drastically from one school to another within municipalities, and for years it has not been possible to equalize them. It is worth mentioning that this whole situation is not education-specific, but reflects the common challenge in Russia of state governance in a vast heterogeneous country.

Despite the large scale of changes covered during reforms, there are at least two critically important *spheres of change that have been neglected*. First, even though it was stated in several strategic documents that there is an observed need for a *minimization of the gap in quality of education among schools* and provision of individual support for schools working in disadvantaged conditions (including schools demonstrating low scores), no measures to reach these results were put in place. Second, the improvement of *teaching practices* was also not given enough attention. The creation of new education standards was not accompanied by the development of new instructional instruments for teachers and new programs for their professional development.

Having made a dramatic leap in the direction of the creation of an institute of independent assessment, Russia failed to form a complementary system for monitoring and analysis of pupils' educational which would allow for the continuous improvement of teaching and learning practices.

It is fair to state that Russia was not unique or alone in the outlined problems that emerged during reforms. In many ways, the Russian case is a vivid embodiment of what Michael Fullan called "the wrong drivers for whole-system reform" (Fullan 2011). It is fair to say, however, that a very large and heterogeneous country succeeded in transitioning from one model of educational governance to a rather different one.

# Some Lessons from Singapore and the Lion

## Oon-Seng Tan

*Oon-Seng Tan is a Chen Yidan Visiting Global Fellow of the Harvard Graduate School Education (HGSE) in 2019. He is a Professor of Education at Nanyang Technological University in Singapore and Director of the Centre for Research in Child Development. Professor Tan was previously Director of the National Institute of Education of Singapore (2014-2018) where he played a significant role in enhancing teacher education and revitalising its training programmes to raise the image and professionalism of teachers. He was previously Dean of Teacher Education where he spearheaded the Teacher Education for the 21st Century (TE21) initiative, a major milestone innovation for teacher education both nationally and internationally. Professor Tan is convener of the World Educational Research Association (WERA) International Research Network on Teacher Education. He has been an Expert Panel Member of the Social Science and Humanities Research for Singapore. He is also an Expert Panel Member of the Tertiary Education Research Funding. He was President of the Educational Research Association of Singapore (ERAS, 2005-2008) and President of the Asia-Pacific Educational Research Association (APERA, 2008-2010). He is Editor-in-Chief of the Educational Research for Policy & Practice (ERPP) journal published by Springer. He is also the Lead Editor of the Asia Pacific Journal of Education (APJE) published by Routledge. Professor Tan was previously board director of several key education agencies including the Singapore Exams and Assessment Board (SEAB), Singapore Centre for Chinese Language (SCCL), and NIE*

*International (NIEI). Professor Tan is also a first board director of the newly established National Institute of Early Childhood Development (NIEC).*


## A Prologue

Since 2008, I have been very privileged to observe close-up the leadership of several very capable education ministers in Singapore owing to my role as a Dean and later as Director of the National Institute of Education (NIE). I have learned tremendously from their insights and decision-making. The NIE despite being an autonomous institution of a globally esteemed research university works in close partnership with the Ministry of Education. Over the last decade Singapore's education system has received unprecedented global interest because of its consistently high performance in cross national assessments of student knowledge and skills such as the Trends in International Mathematics and Science Study (TIMSS), and the Progress in International Reading Literacy Study (PIRLS) both administered by the International Association for the Evaluation of Educational Achievement, and most recently the Programme for International Student Assessment (PISA) of the Organization for Economic Cooperation and Development. Sparked by Singapore's high performance on those students Ministerial delegations from all over the world have visited Singapore and the NIE, and I have had the privilege of meeting numerous education ministers from Asia, Europe, and North and South America. Very often, the visiting ministers would engage me on many issues, such as getting policies right regarding class size, identifying levers to raise student performance, producing effective teachers, and equipping students for 21st century skills. Thanks to the OECD's reports on education, I have also had the privilege of meeting many ministers of education at international summits to share my academic perspective of the Singapore case. Most recently, I met an education politician from Europe who asked me where does one begin if there were many things to fix in education. In this brief document I synthesize the advice I would give a new minister of education.

## Education is for the Long Haul

Education is for the long haul, and the quality of education impacts nation-building, values preservation, and people's capacity for adaption, value creation and innovation.

Dear Minister, please allow me to recommend that you read *Lee Kuan Yew's Educational Legacy* (Tan, Low and Hung, 2017). When Singapore gained independence in 1965, its leaders were confronted with the task of nation-building in a country which was a picture of poverty with hardly any natural resources and plagued by issues such as tensions along ethnic fault-lines. In 1966, Lee Kuan Yew gathered a group of educators and said to them: "I have really come to discuss a problem with you, a problem which can be solved only, when ultimately not I, the Ministry officials or you understand it, but when the teacher understands it. Because the most important digit in what we are trying to do is the teacher. There are two factors in the formative influences of a young man or young woman's life: one is the home; the

155

other is the school. We cannot do very much about the home, but we can do something about the school" (Lee, 1966).

The late founding Prime Minister of Singapore Lee Kuan Yew once remarked that the education ministerial position is "not the most popular of portfolios" and a "job where angels fear to tread" (Lee, 1977). It is not the grandiose slogans of alleviating poverty or charismatic statements of social justice and human rights that will turn societies around, but patience and    perseverance with great intentionality and temerity that bring about a nation's progress.

The values that ensured Singapore's meteoric rate of advancement are not necessarily unique. Recently, I was at Stavanger, a city in Norway that was once upon a time a fishing village subject to the tough Nordic weather. Today people think of Norway as a nation with oil wealth, not to mention beautiful fjords, mountains, and the midnight sun. Without oil, the country would not have had the resources available to make the great wonders of nature accessible to everyone. However, oil money did not just come easily with the discovery of the offshore oil beds. In the autumn of 1969, the Ocean Viking drilling rig discovered crude oil in the Norwegian continental shelf. At that time, however, producing oil in rough seas was so challenging as to be almost humanly impossible. People needed to come together with a vision for the long-haul gains from the oil discovery. The Norwegians were blessed with pioneers who had integrity, intelligence and innovation. For example, new technologies had to be developed, such as the building of

156

giant concrete platforms and the installation of underwater structures and extensive pipelines in deep waters.

Like the early Norwegians, the pioneers of Singapore, too, began with the right leadership and collaborative values focused on the long-term. Education should be values-driven and must never be short-sighted. In the case of Singapore, responsiveness to changing local and global landscapes and commitment to ensure the highest standards of quality is critical. We need to learn productivity from the Norwegians. At the Stavanger Petroleum Museum I learned that the nature of offshore oil extraction is such that only a small proportion of oil can be extracted out of every seabed. Worldwide, the average extraction rate for similar ventures is 25-30 percent. To be better than that, one needs sophisticated and efficient use of technology, as well as highly trained and motivated workers that range from engineers to chemists and divers. For Norway, the average recovery factor far exceeds that of many countries at a rate of 46 percent. The Norwegian appreciates the value of just 1 percent more extraction as every extra 1 percent would be worth an additional 300 billion NOK! Likewise, education must produce people with a mind-set of excellence characterised by using the best machines with the highest human motivation.

Likewise, educational developments, whilst geared towards responding to the economic and social needs of the people, must continue to keep abreast with the latest technological innovations. We should also ensure that much learning is extracted out of each hour spent in school by every child. Our teachers should understand how each student learns best and be very intentional in providing for much meaningful learning that propels the student to be deeply knowledgeable and to learn how to learn. Beyond economic interest, there is the need to maintain an educational system that adopts a holistic approach which preserves national culture, identity, and values rooted in family and community.

I have three words of advice for a new education minister: Legacy, People and Future. I believe good education ministers pay attention to the strengths of the system and take a "building-block" approach, while reforming and transforming different parts of the system. There are 3Ps for education leaders to reflect on: **P**aradigms (Worldviews and Perspectives), **P**hilosophy (Beliefs), and **P**racticality (What do you want to do?). Our worldview must be both "telescopic" and "helicopter" in nature. By telescopic I mean understanding the past (where we came from and how we arrived at the present) and seeing into the future (intelligent extrapolation). We also need a helicopter view of things: rising above micro and fragmentary issues and having a big picture of things. Paradigms refer to our understanding of conflicting worldviews and shifting underlying assumptions. All the different stakeholders of education have their own assumptions. What is your vision of where education is heading? Do you believe that education can change the fate of many, especially those caught in the poverty cycle? How can we ensure equal opportunity for every child regardless of background? Are we correctly allocating our limited resources between investing in higher education and investing in early childhood education?

Education must be future-oriented. Education leaders need to be cognizant of the changing nature of knowledge, learning, and environments. Teachers are to be facilitators of learning and designers of the learning environment. Teachers need to embrace new pedagogies and transform pedagogical practices, for example, to account for new ways in which learners gain information through technology and social media. Teachers must appreciate their role in cultivating 21st century competencies including problem-solving, critical thinking, collaboration, creativity, and interpersonal skills. These things are not difficult – just think BIG and MAD. Encourage curriculum shifts that promote (i) **B**ig-picture thinking (there are already lots of pedagogies for this, ranging from project work to problem-based learning); (ii) **I**nquiry (re-instilling the sense of curiosity in students); and (iii) **G**rit (positive emotions and resilience in the face of difficulty should be cultivated). Foster (i) **M**ultiple perspective-taking; (ii) **A**ccomplishments more than assessment (i.e. authentic real-world learning and accomplishments that impact people and society); and (iii) **D**ialogue (engagement that sharpens the visibility of students' thinking, rather than just the teacher's).

**Trusting Teachers: Ten Commandments of Teacher Policy**
Dear Minister, I often ask students what their best teachers in school are like. The answer I get most often is "caring teachers". A good education system is made up of caring teachers. When teachers are asked what they want most from the Ministry, the response that invariably comes up is

"trust". We need to trust teachers and develop teacher polices for this to happen.

Please allow me to share "Ten Commandments" of effective teacher policies.

First commandment: Recruit quality candidates. Attract people with the right balance of aptitude and attitude. Aptitude includes subject proficiency and good communication skills, and attitude must be characterised by a genuine love of working with children or youth. Put these candidates through internships and the like so they can benefit from authentic classroom experience.

Second commandment: Understand the reasons why people do not want to be teachers. Address altruistic, intrinsic and extrinsic factors. Ensuring competitive salaries for teachers is essential, and policymakers should benchmark salaries appropriately. Raising salaries above the market average does not necessarily lead to substantial increases in quality. It is better to provide competitive salaries and make room for the best to progress towards higher salary scales through built-in merit increments. Provide incentives such as leave for professional and personal growth.

Third commandment: Build a quality initial teacher education program and incorporate high standards of teacher accreditation. The best teacher education programs are holistic, and include both general and specialized content knowledge training, with a substantial focus on research-informed pedagogy. They also integrate theory and practice effectively, and facilitate the growth of strong learning communities. Furthermore, they incorporate mentoring with experienced teachers working collaboratively with teacher educators who are well-versed in education research.

Fourth commandment: Give teachers a vision of their career pathway. Education is becoming an increasingly complex enterprise and sophisticated expertise is needed in pedagogy, curriculum development, and leadership of educational units. Facilitate the creation of career tracks to provide opportunities for career progression and talent allocation. Different tracks should be carved out for teachers to become master teachers, curriculum experts and school leaders. Clearer professional pathways also signal professional authority and autonomy amongst teaching professionals.

Fifth commandment: Support teachers with continuous learning and professional growth. Teachers must keep up-to-date with new knowledge, skills and teaching practices. Professional development goes beyond workshops and courses, to include school-embedded professional development, sophisticated induction and mentoring, collaborative teacher networks and project-based research-cum-inquiry approaches to improve teaching practices and learning outcomes.

Sixth commandment: Establish a growth mindset of accountability and evaluation. We want teachers to do professional self-evaluation with a perspective on how can they can do an even better job to impact student holistic development and learning outcomes.

Seventh commandment: Establish a succession of strong school leadership. School leadership plays a critical role in transforming the environment in which teachers and learners function. Pay attention to the selection of school leaders, promote effective leadership practices and the development of leadership capacity. Proactive approaches and succession planning are essential.

Eighth commandment: Promote the teacher's image. Our vision of teachers must go beyond them being mere communicators of content, to encompass their roles as leaders in pedagogical thinking, inspirational role models, respected domain experts, and custodians of societal values. Key policy factors in enhancing teacher symbolism include: (i) building cultural regard for teachers; (ii) making space for professional autonomy and trust; (iii) publicizing the good work of teachers; (iv) managing workloads and the general working environment; (v) giving national recognition for the accomplishments of teaching professionals; and (vi) utilizing branding and marketing campaigns to raise the attractiveness of the profession.

Ninth commandment: Ensure coherence for effective implementation. Remember the whole is more than the sum of its parts when it comes to effective policy implementation. Effective education systems have a "big-picture" perspective and coordinate policies with a view to longer-term impact. Key policy strategies include: (i) governance structures that ensure alignment of activities and optimization of resources; (ii) collaboration among all stakeholders; and (iii) the presence of mediating layers and networks for facilitating implementation.

Tenth commandment: Listen to the teacher's voice. Teachers are at the frontline of education challenges. The teacher factor trumps everything else in ensuring high student outcomes. They also sense the pulse of the next generation. Go beyond education data and have first- hand dialogue with teachers. Dedicated teachers often go the extra mile in spotting students who lag behind because of learning difficulties. The teacher factor, unlike other systemic factors, is different – because it is the human factor. Moreover, teachers play vital roles not only in ensuring strong academic foundations in fundamental literacies such as verbal and quantitative skills and reasoning abilities, but also in inspiring, motivating, mentoring and facilitating every student's search for knowledge. Teachers are also key players in anchoring the ethos and values of society. In a very real and tangible way, teachers are –for better or worse– the role models students look up to, given that they are the adults with whom children and teenagers spend a large part of their lives with outside of the family context.

**Learning from the Lion**

The name "Singapore" came from the word "Singa-pura" which means "Lion-city". The legend is a long story so you need to visit Singapore to understand the myth. However, every new Minister of Education should go on an African Safari to learn from the lion. I was in South Africa to give a keynote at a conference and went for my "lion lesson". The African Safari provides fascinating insights into how the lion survives and what parallel lessons can be drawn for education. I learnt that the lion must be focused when it comes to hunting for its prey; each time the lion goes out to get food, it must ensure it gets its target as it cannot afford to have its energy depleted in a fruitless outing. Imagine if each time the lion goes for an antelope, he misses his catch. This will not only leave him hungry, but will also render him weak as his muscles will have atrophied in his failed attempt to nab his prey. Lions cannot survive on vegetation – they are carnivorous. In fact, when lions are weak and cannot run, they become a target for the other predators.

Similarly, Education Ministers need to be very focused in what they want to achieve and deploy their limited energies and resources to "fight the right battles" and to "make the main thing the main thing", so to speak. Education Ministers need to have the wisdom to decide on what they can achieve during their tenure, and with perseverance see through its successful implementation. The lion is king only because it is highly strategic!

I also gleaned another insight from the behavior of the lion. During our guided Safari tours, our rangers drove us through the expansive terrain in their sturdy 4X4 Open Game Drive vehicles. We were told to never stand up in the vehicle and as long as we remained seated, the animal would never attack us even though it may come within close proximity to our vehicle. This is because the vision of the lion differs from that of humans. Lions don't see things the way we do. Remember that your stakeholders don't see things from your perspective. When you are seated in the Safari vehicle, the lion cannot see the individuals in the vehicle. His eyes only see a massive vehicle before them. Being strategic about his resource expenditure, the lion will not take on a tougher and larger animal so he will not even bother with the vehicle. Well, that's so long as we remain seated in the vehicle. But the moment any individual chooses to separate himself from the vehicle, the lion will grab that individual human – as it happened recently to a tourist who, ignoring the reminder of the ranger, jumped out of a Safari vehicle to take photos. Similarly, Education Ministers need to see they are a part of a larger community. There is no room for personal ego or agenda, but the interests of students, teachers, principals, parents and the society at large, who are all stakeholders together with you.

Thank you for reading. I wish you the very best.

## References

Lee, K.Y. (1966). *Transcript of speech by the Prime Minister at a meeting with principals of schools at the Victoria Theatre on 29th August 1966.* Singapore: National Archives of Singapore.

Lee, K.Y. (1977). *Speech by Prime Minister Lee Kuan Yew, in parliament on 23rd February 1977.* Singapore: National Archives of Singapore.

Tan, O.S., Low, E.L. and Hung, D. (2017). Lee Kuan Yew's Educational Legacy: The Challenges of Success. Singapore: Springer Nature.

Made in the USA
Middletown, DE
14 February 2019